VIOLINJUDY'S
A VIOLIN WORKBOOK

NOTE READING AND FINGERING WORKSHEETS
FOR BEGINNING
VIOLIN STUDENTS

VERY FUN VIOLIN COLLECTION

A Violin WorkBook by Judy Naillon
Copyright © 2023 ViolinJudy
www.violinjudy.com
ISBN:978-1-960674-18-0

All Rights Reserved. This book or parts thereof may not be reproduced in any form, stored in any retrieval system, or transmitted in any form by any means-eletronic, mechanical, photocopy, recording, or otherwise - without prior written permission or the publisher, except as provided by copyright law.

VERY FUN VIOLIN LIBRARY

A *Violin Workbook* is designed *for* violin students in levels A-B.
A book level chart for the *Very Fun Violin Collection* is provided at the end of this book.

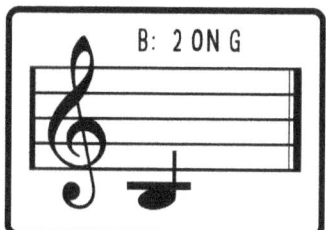
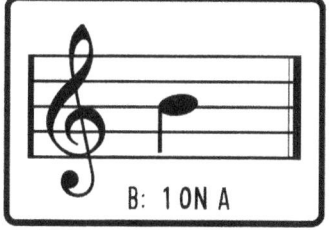

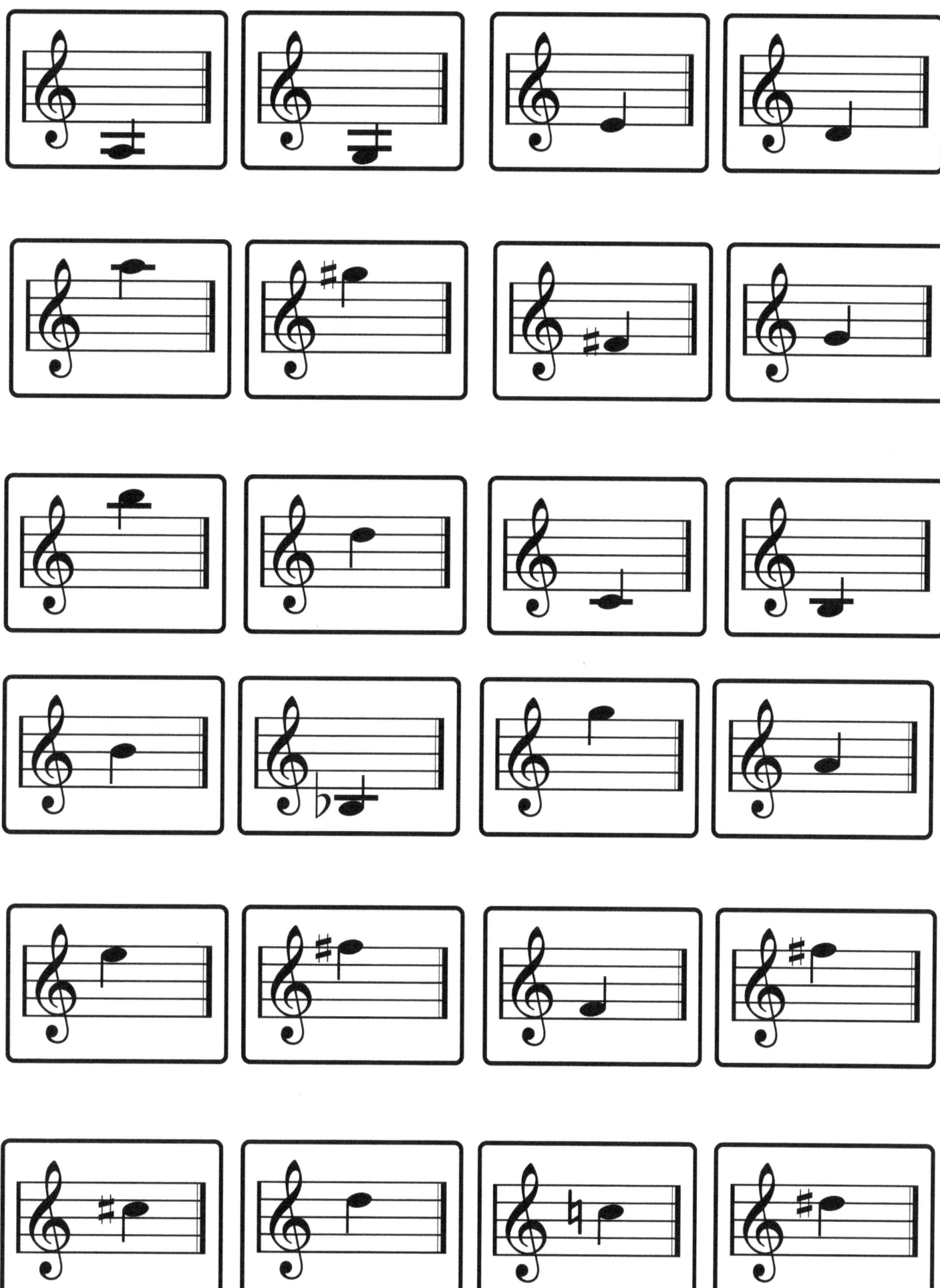

TREBLE CLEF VIOLIN OPEN STRINGS

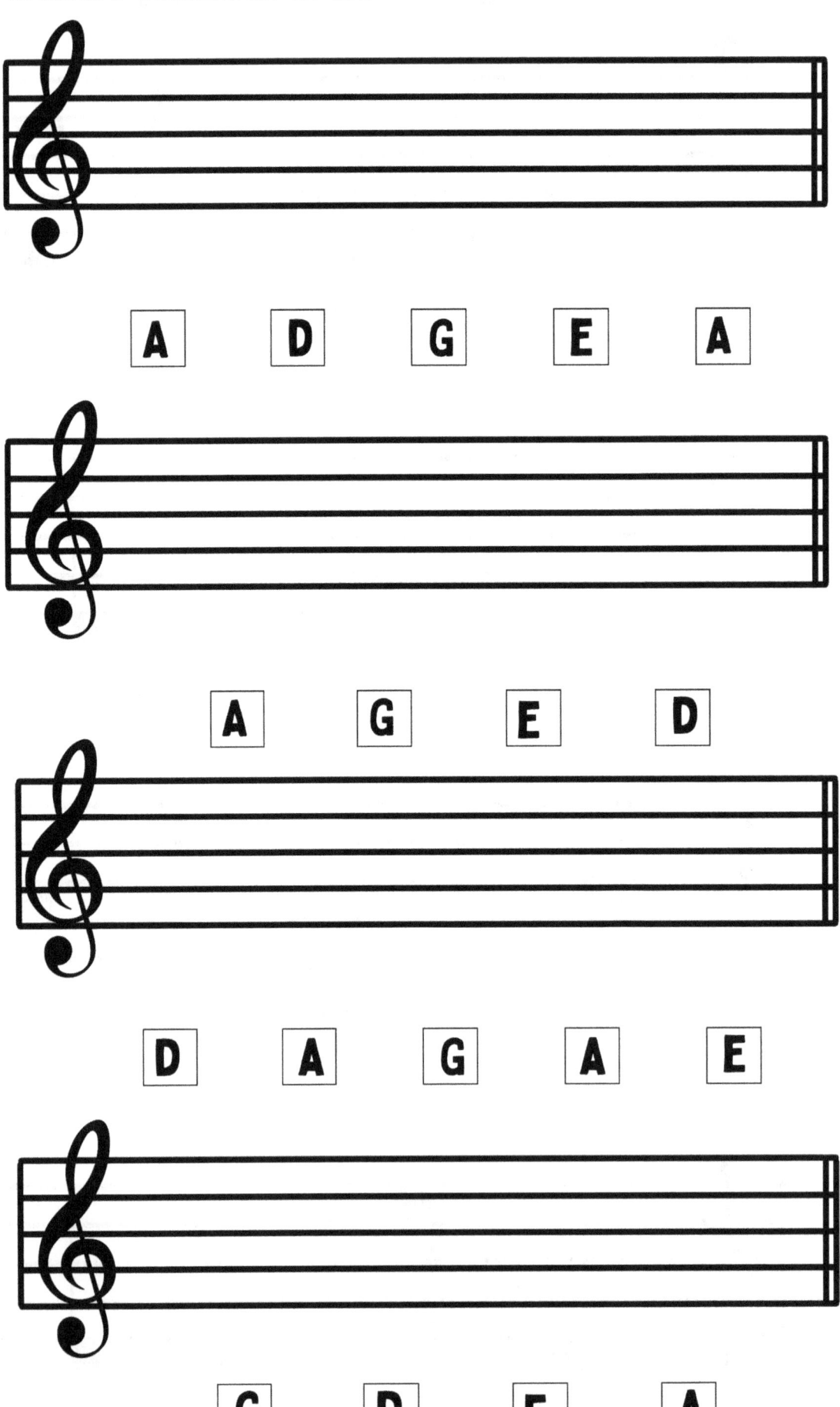

TREBLE CLEF LINE & SPACE NOTES

DRAW TREBLE CLEF LINE & SPACE NOTES

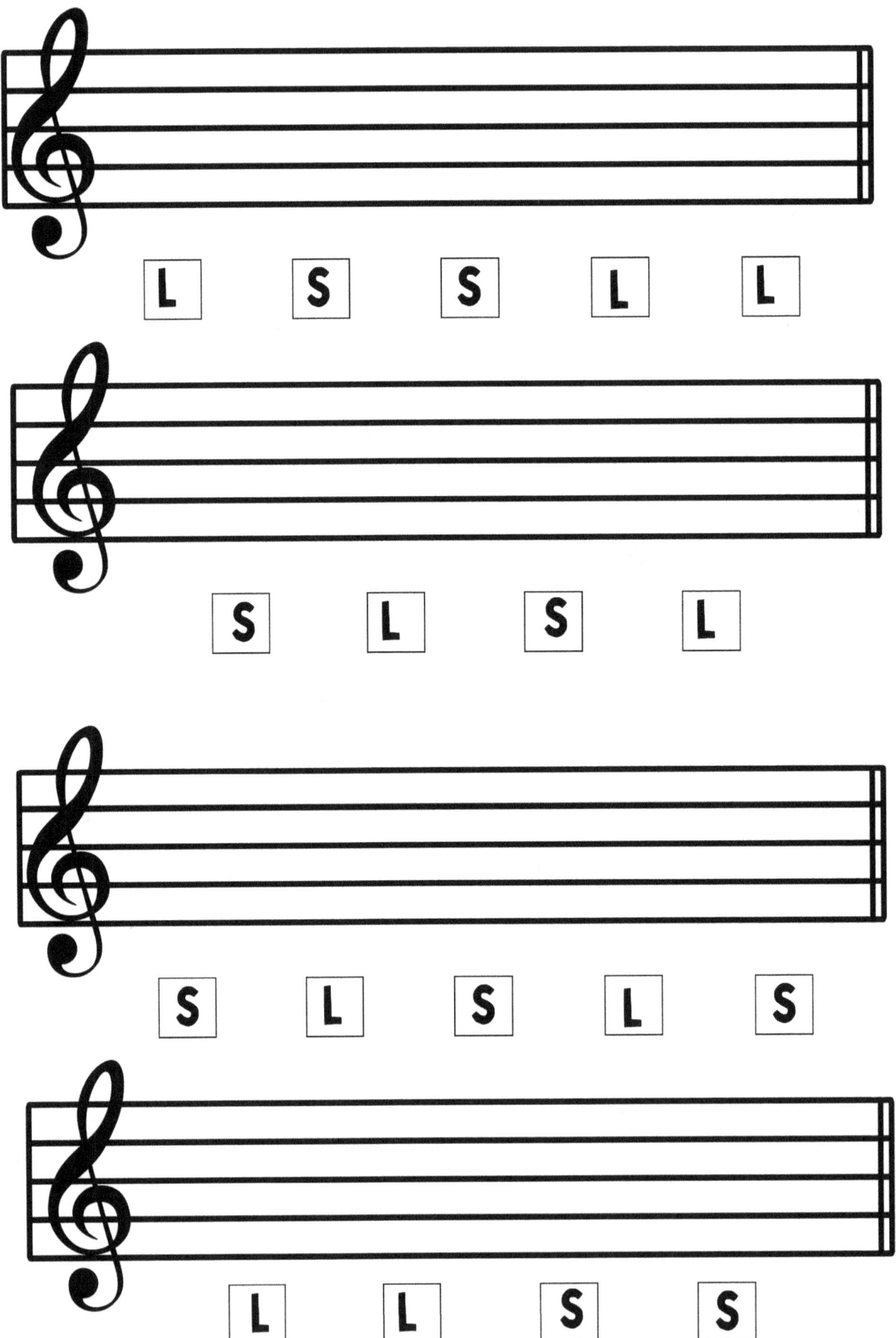

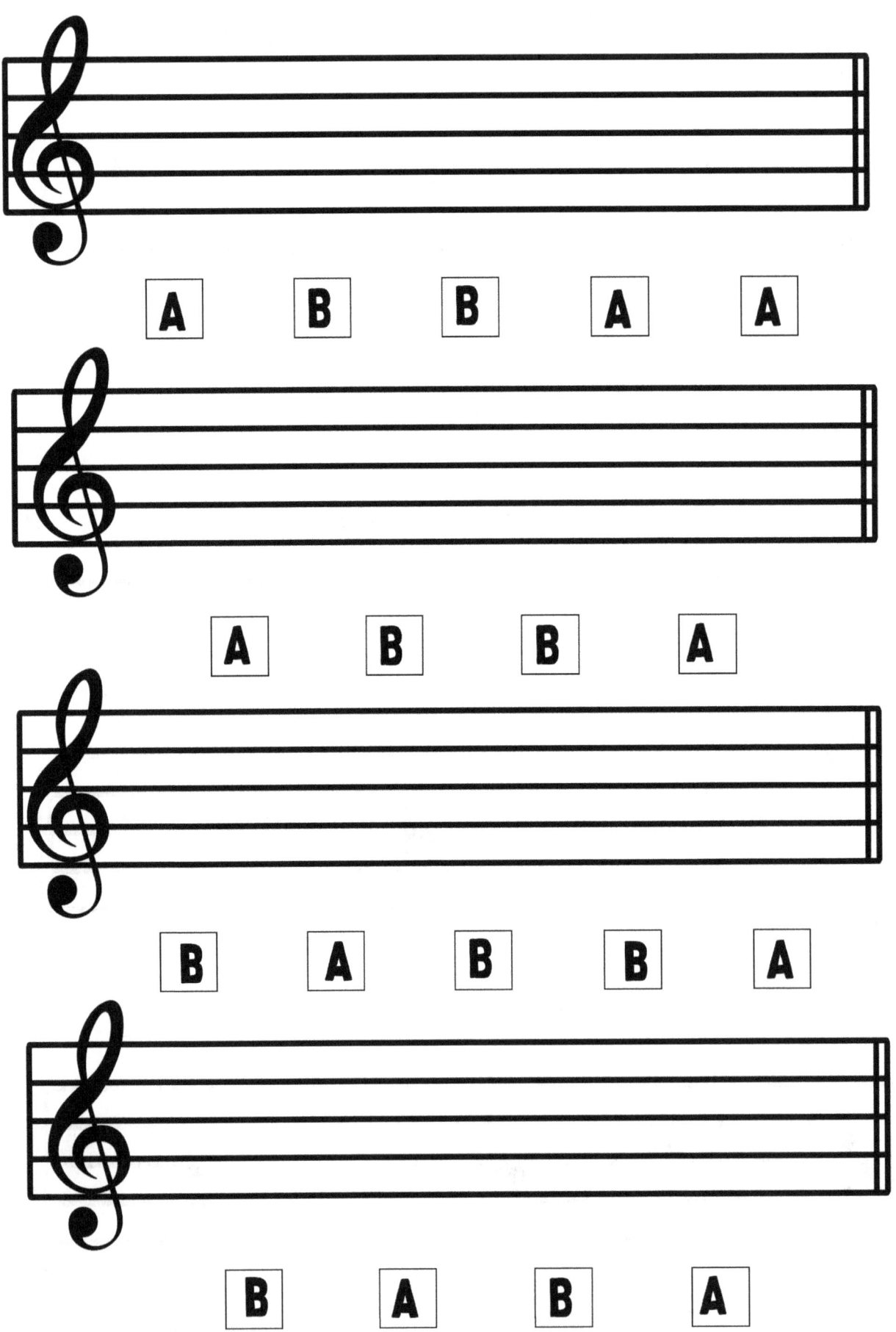

TREBLE CLEF A, B & C

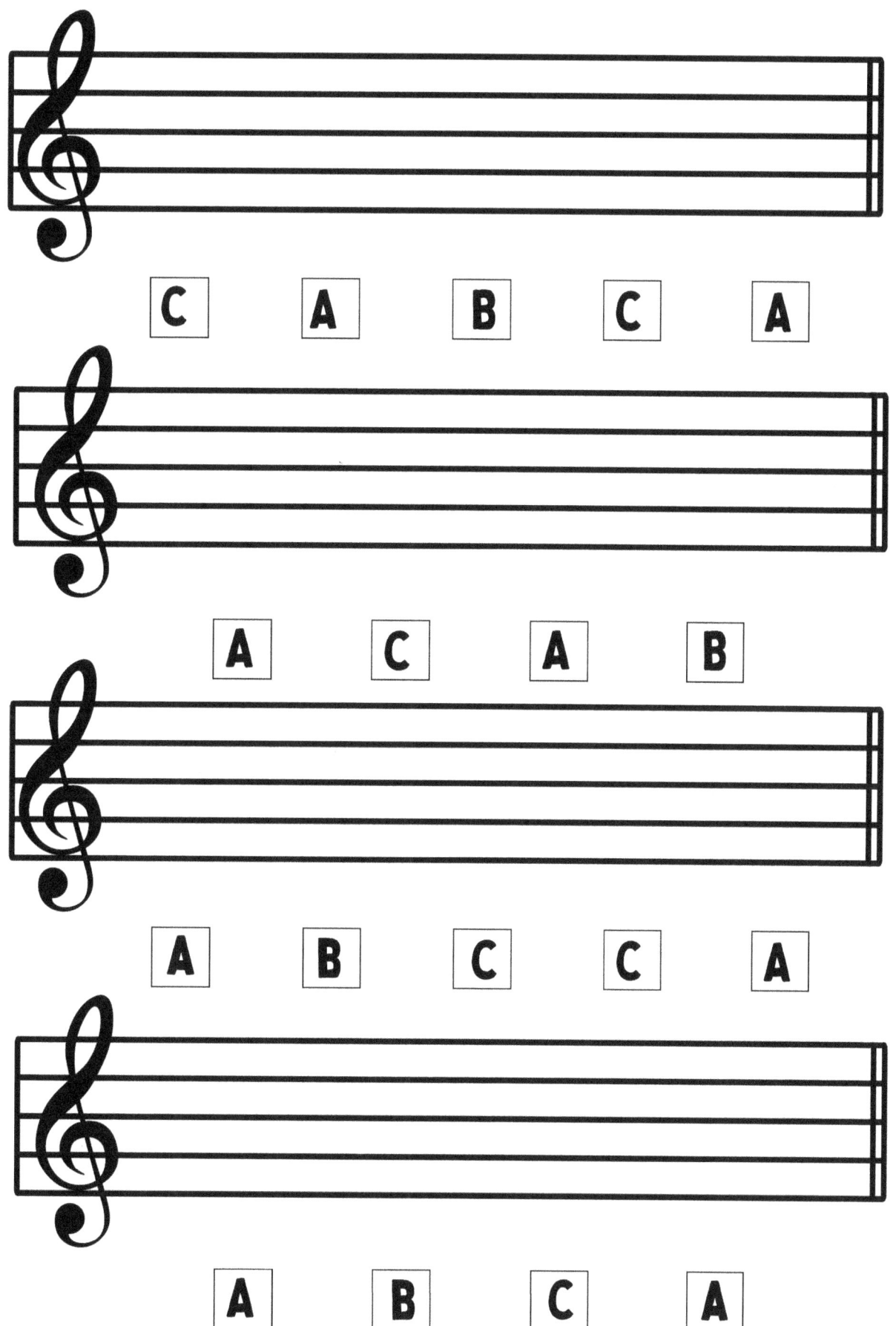

VIOLIN OPEN A, 1 ON A, 2 ON A

TREBLE CLEF A, B, C, D

DRAW TREBLE CLEF A, B, C & D

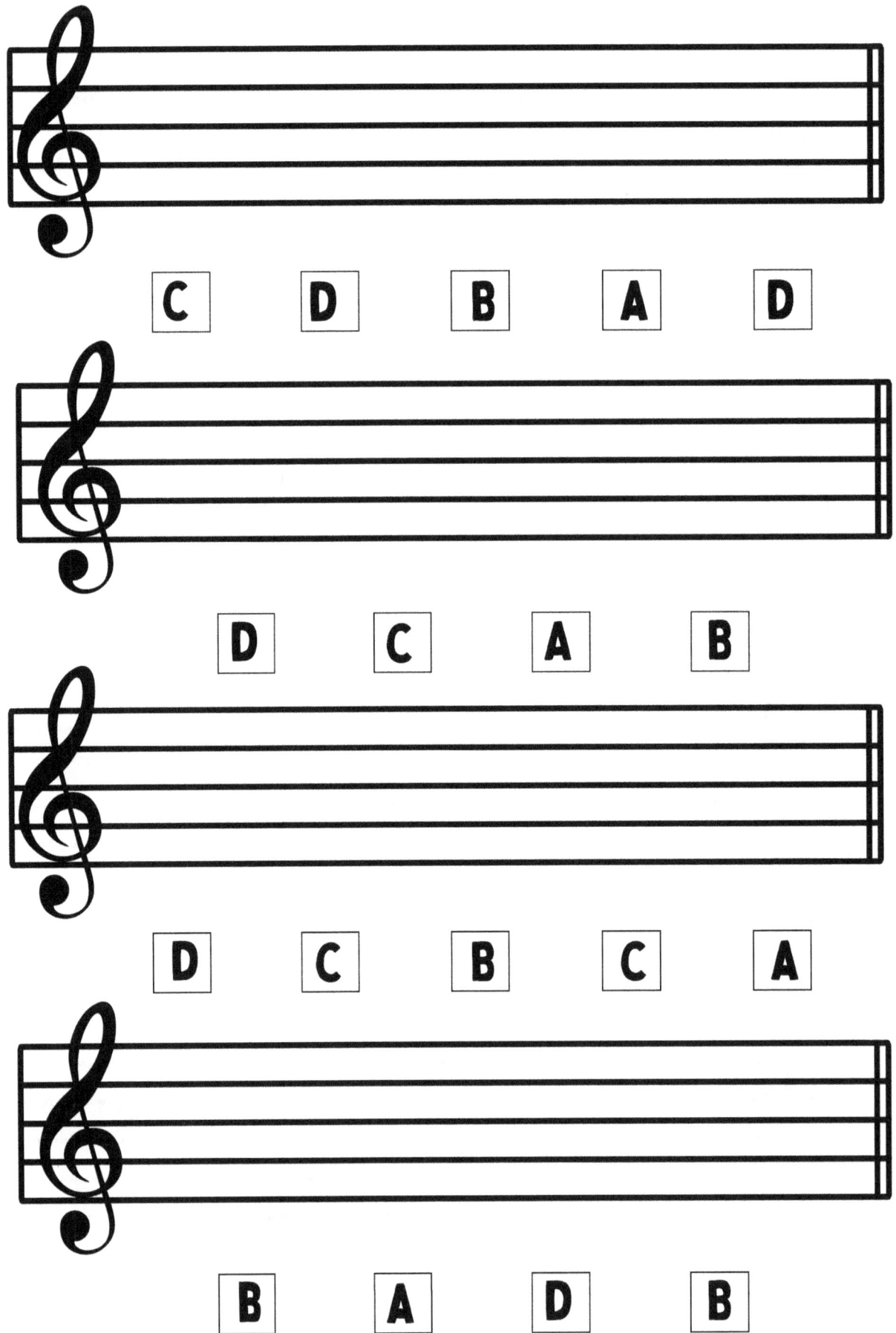

TREBLE CLEF E, F

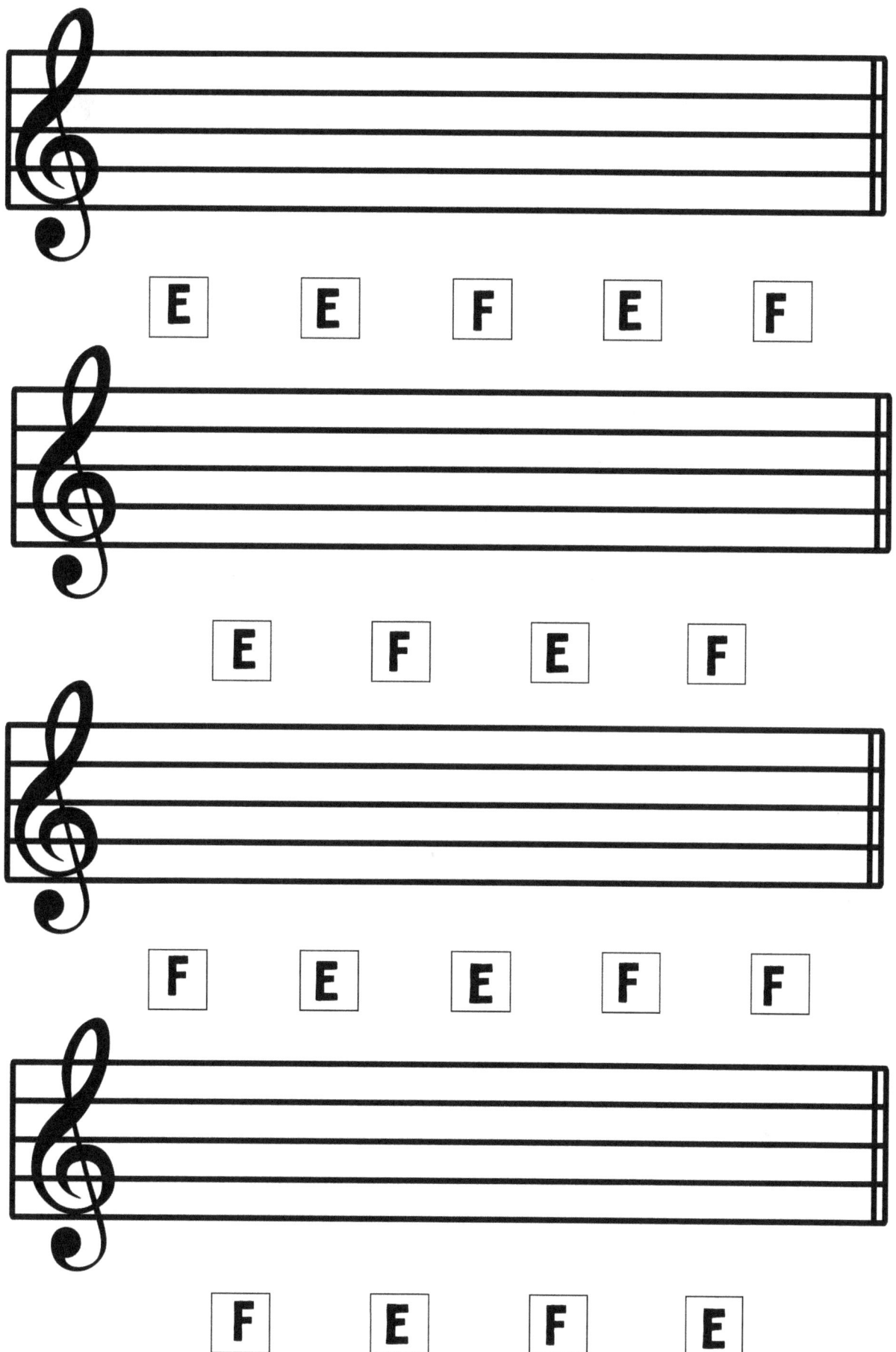

VIOLIN 1 ON E, OPEN E

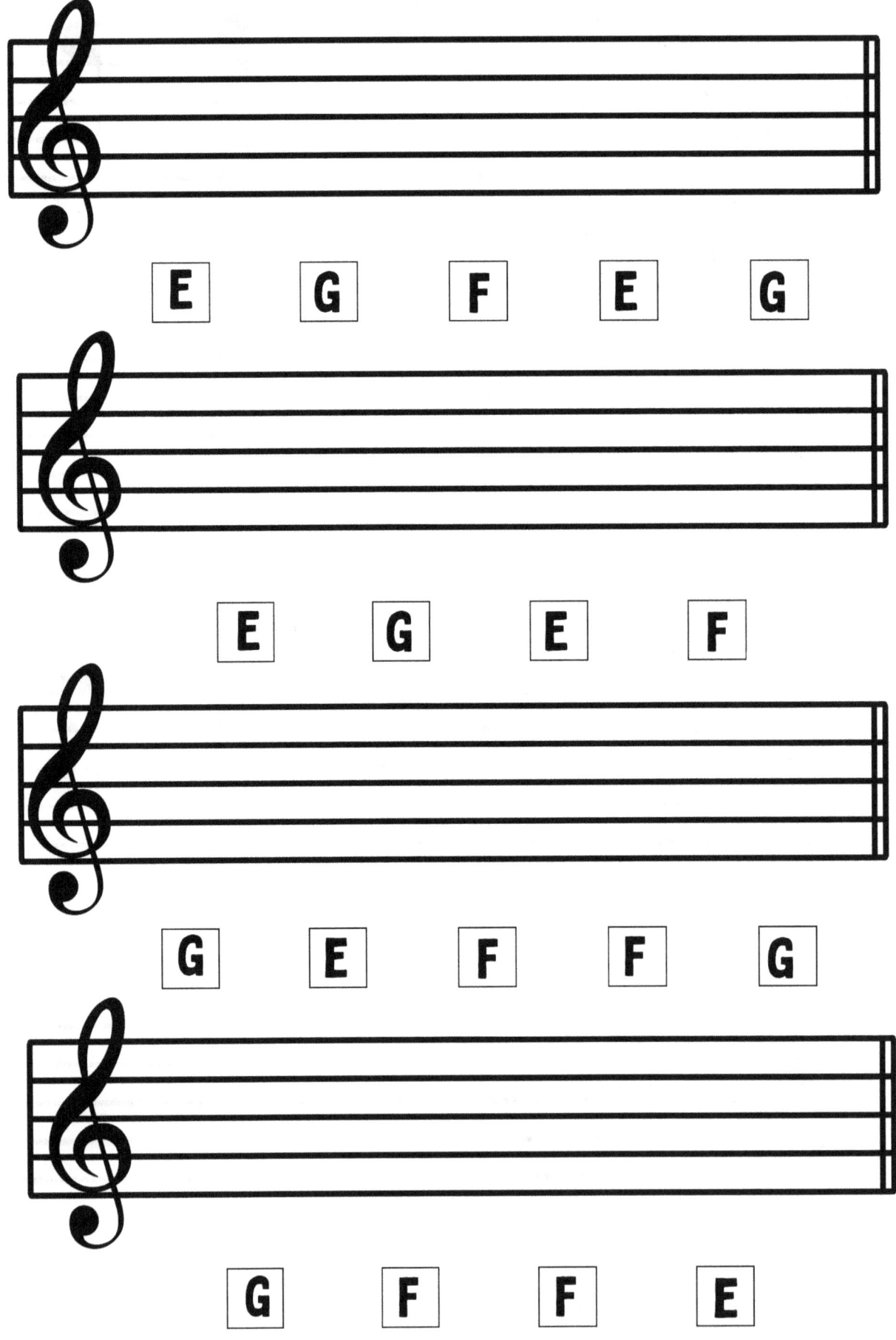

VIOLIN OPEN E, 1 ON E OR 2 ON E

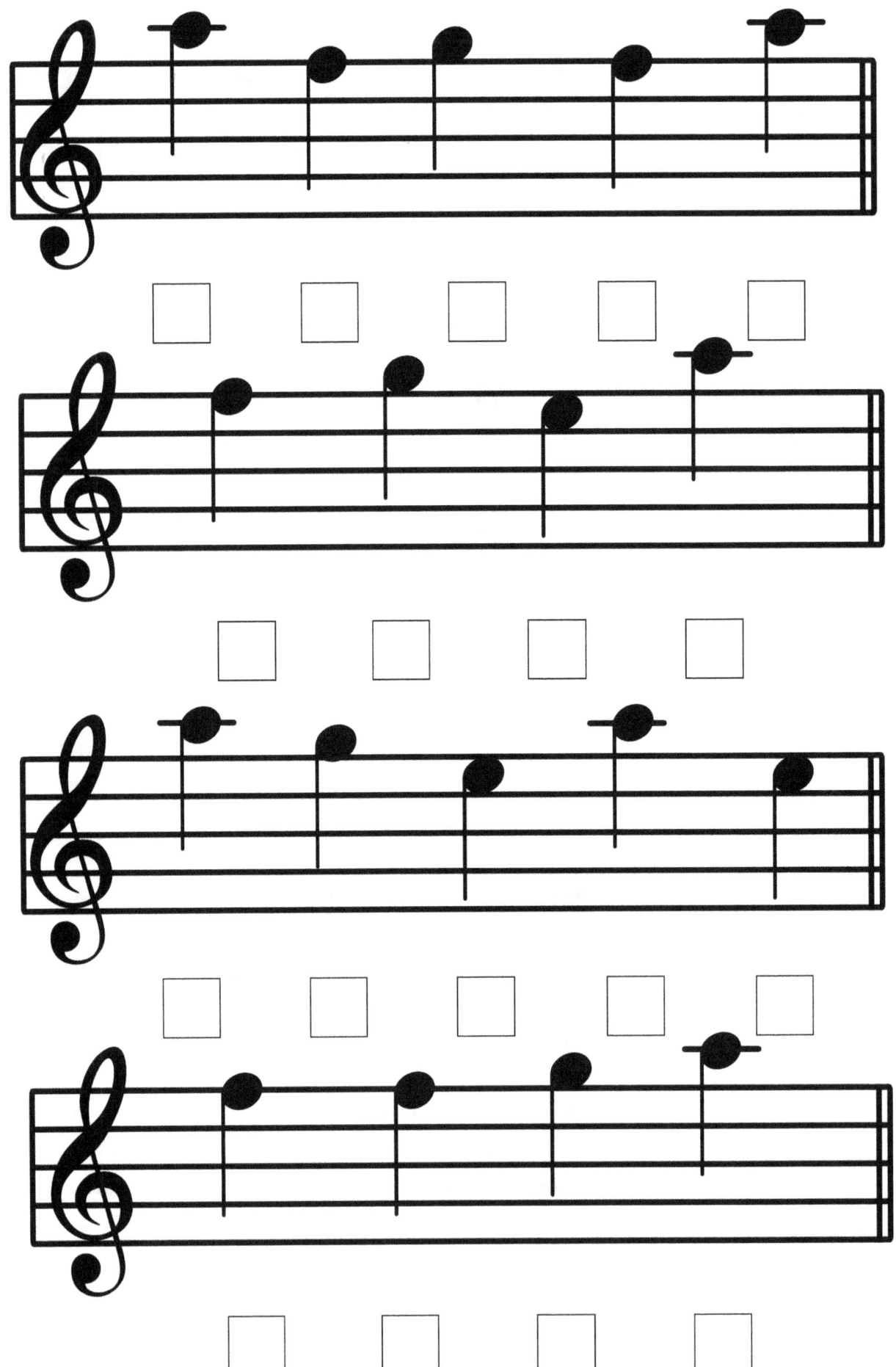

DRAW TREBLE CLEF E, F, G, A

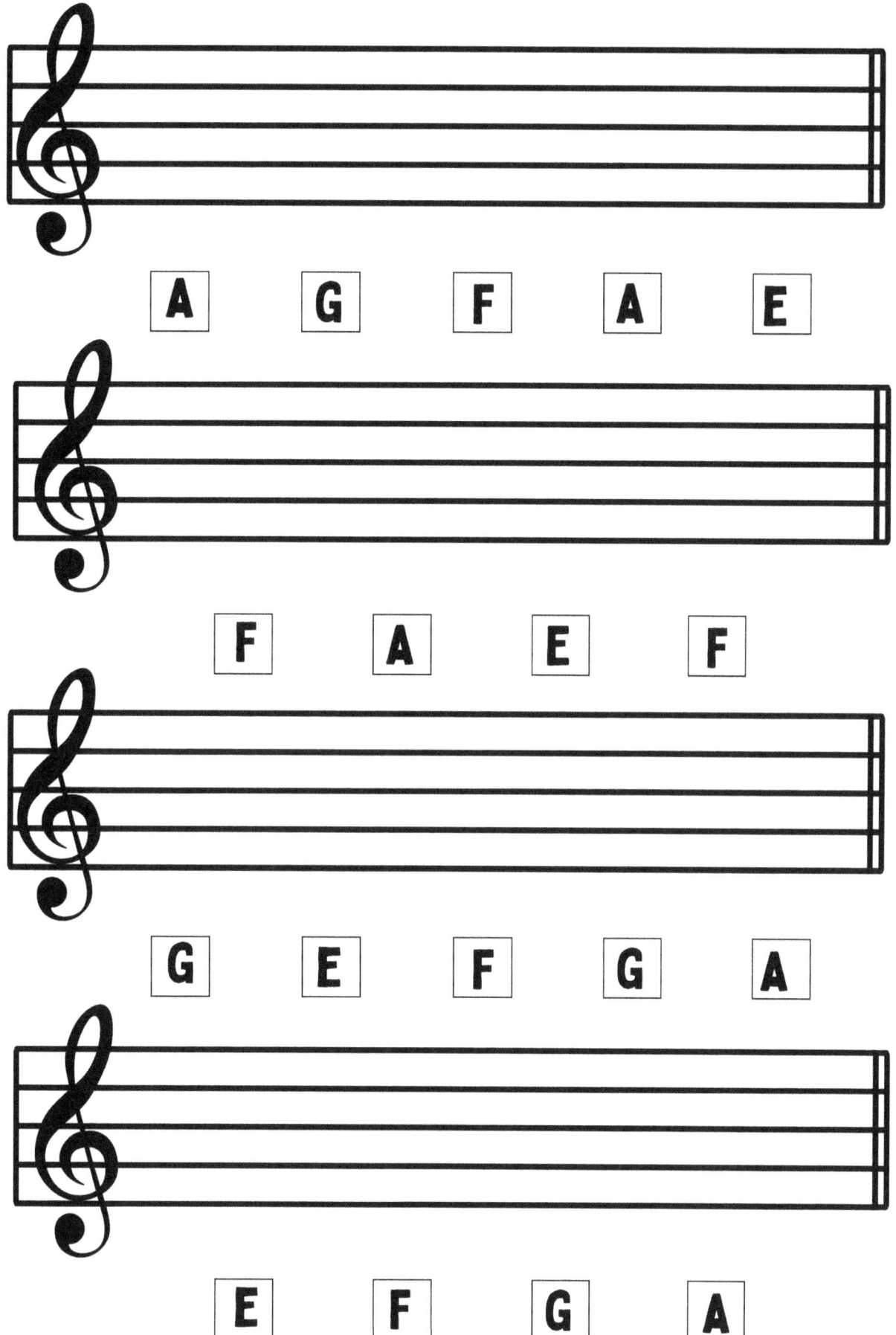

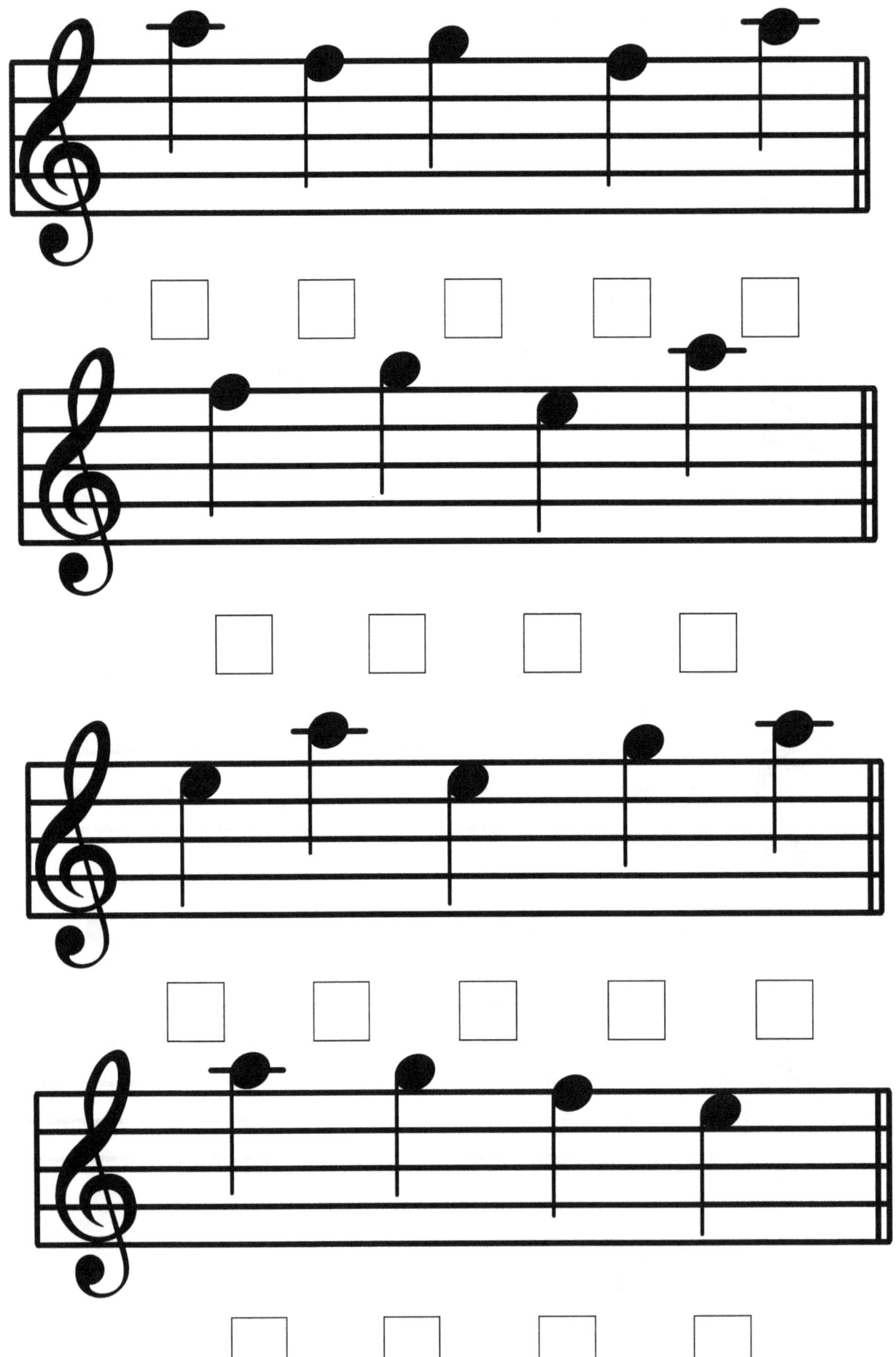

TREBLE CLEF E, F, G, A, B

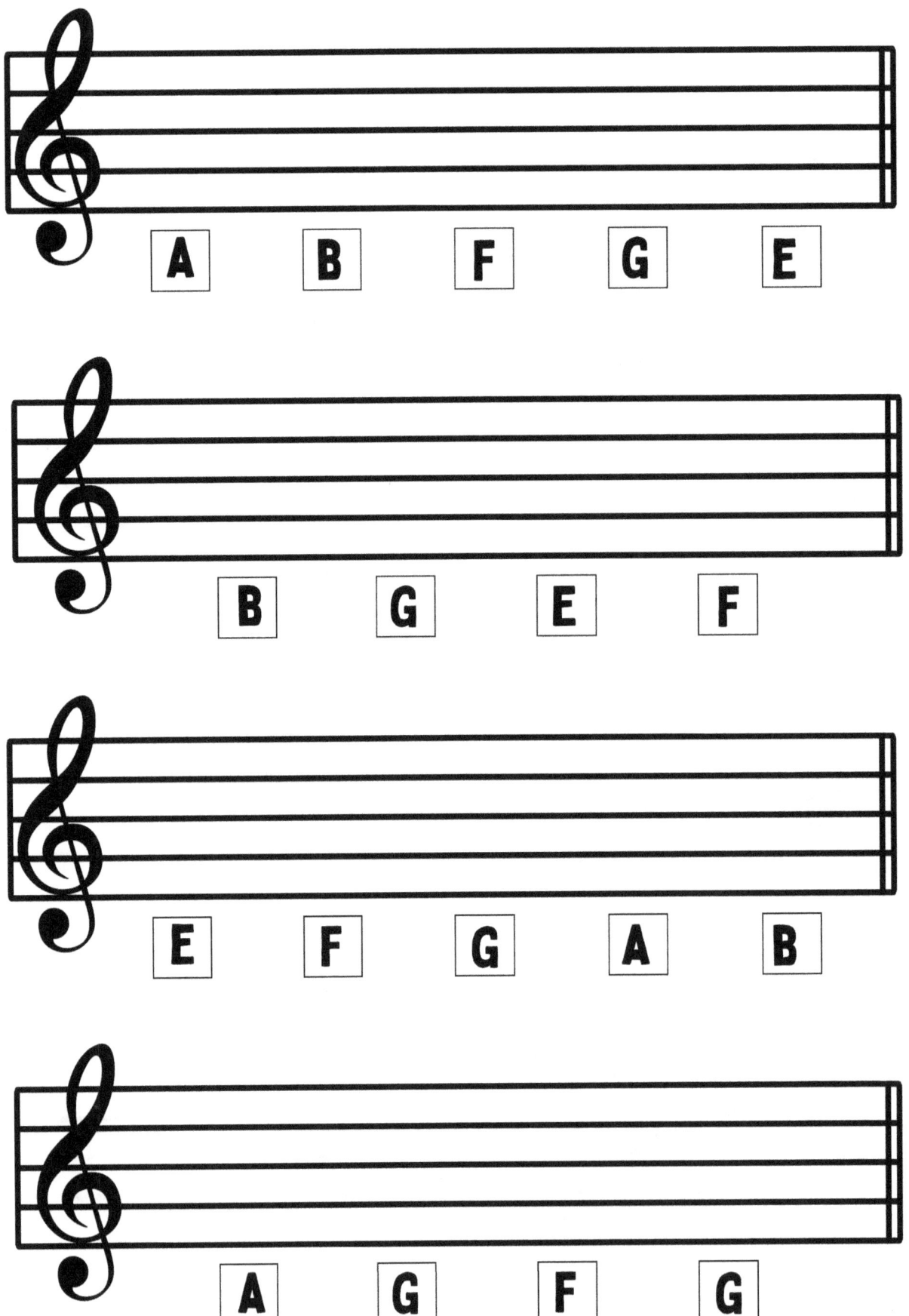

VIOLIN OPEN E, 1, 2, 3, 4 ON E

TREBLE CLEF D & E

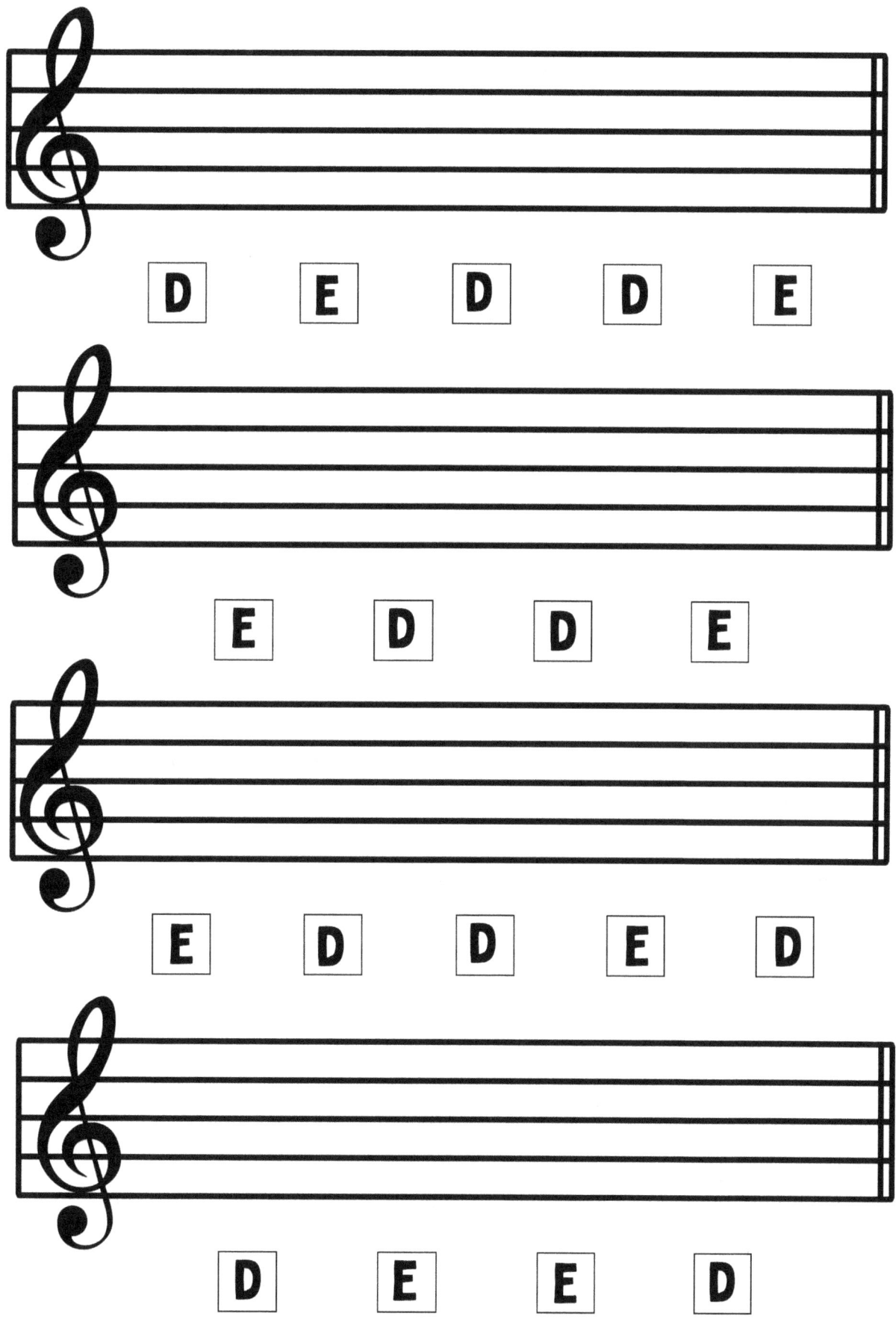

VIOLIN OPEN D STRING & 1 ON D

TREBLE CLEF D, E & F

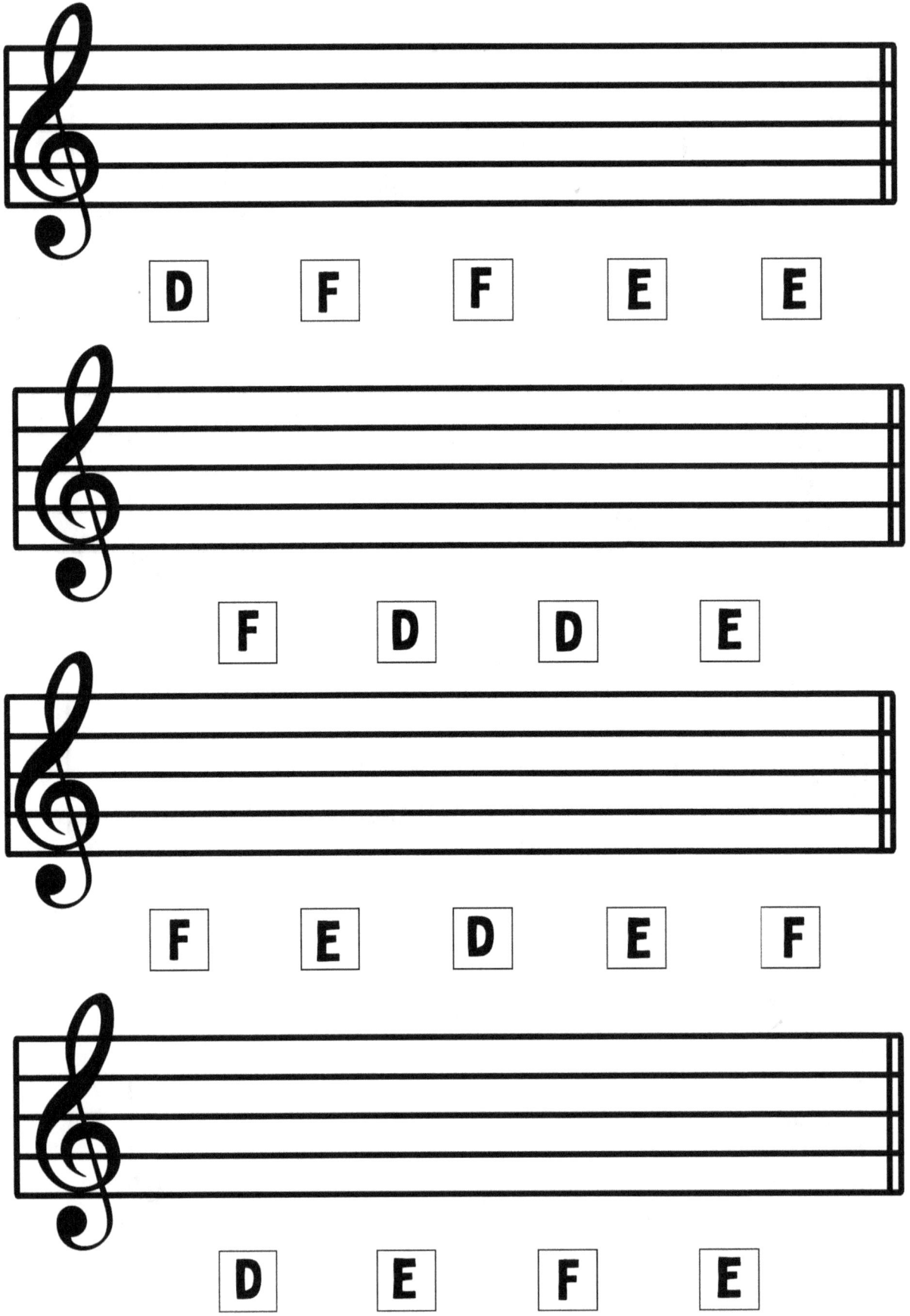

VIOLIN OPEN D, 1, 2 ON D STRING

TREBLE D, E, F & G

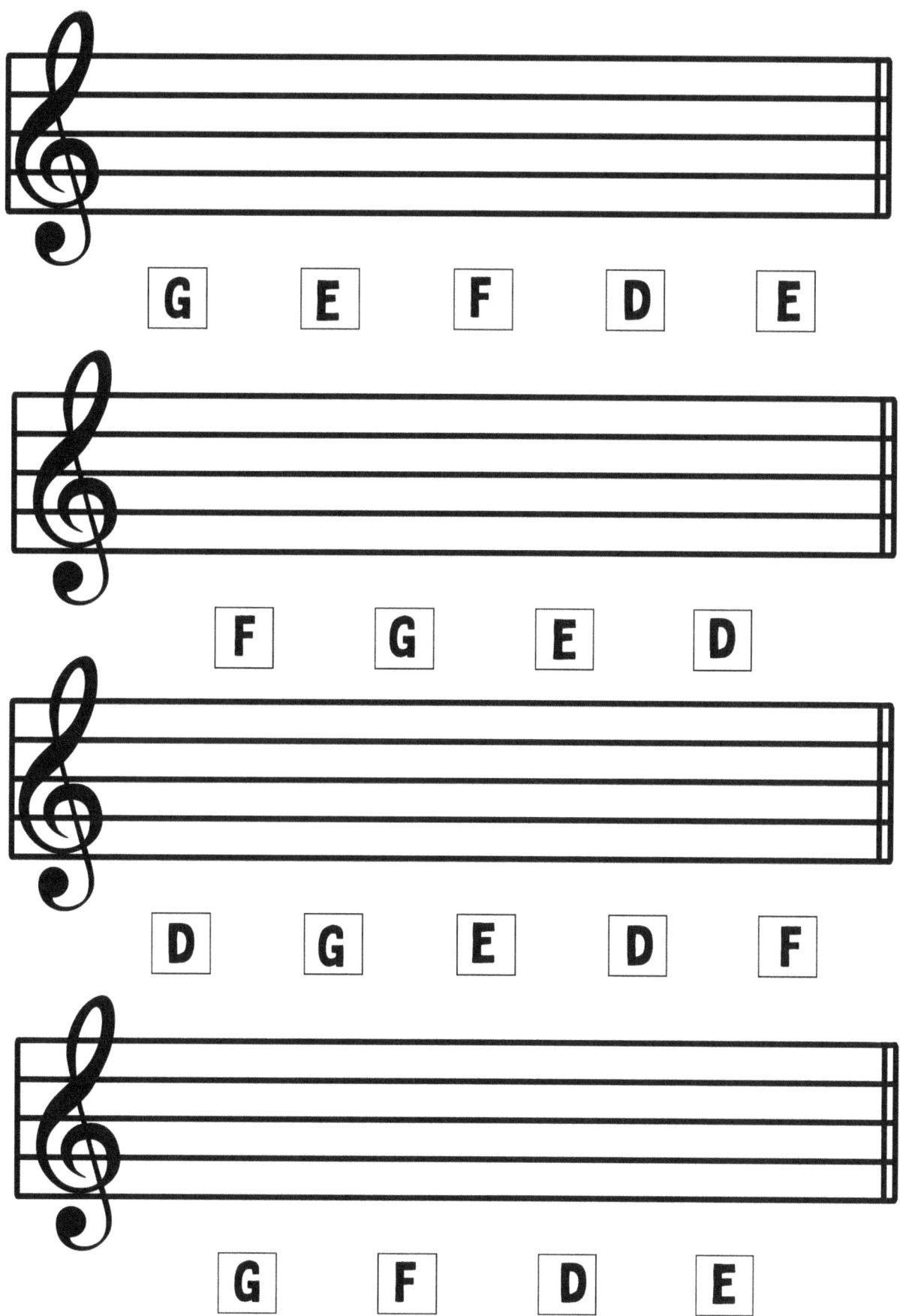

VIOLIN OPEN D, 1, 2, 3 ON D

TREBLE G & A

WRITE TREBLE CLEF G & A

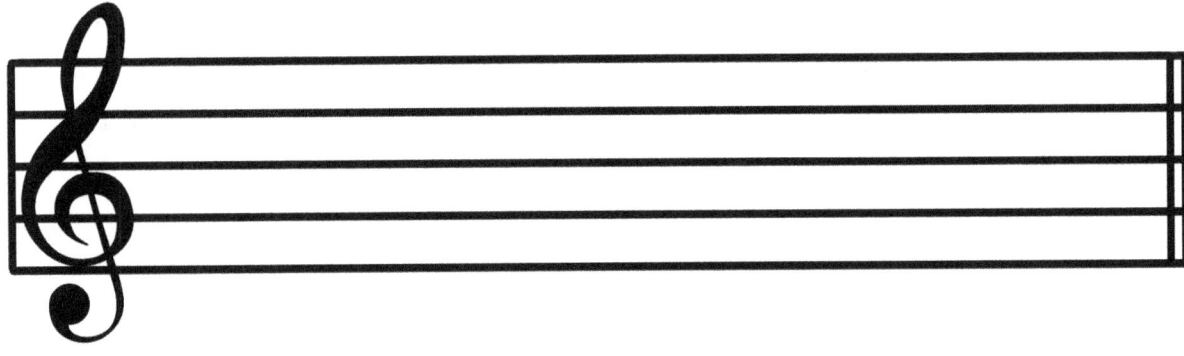

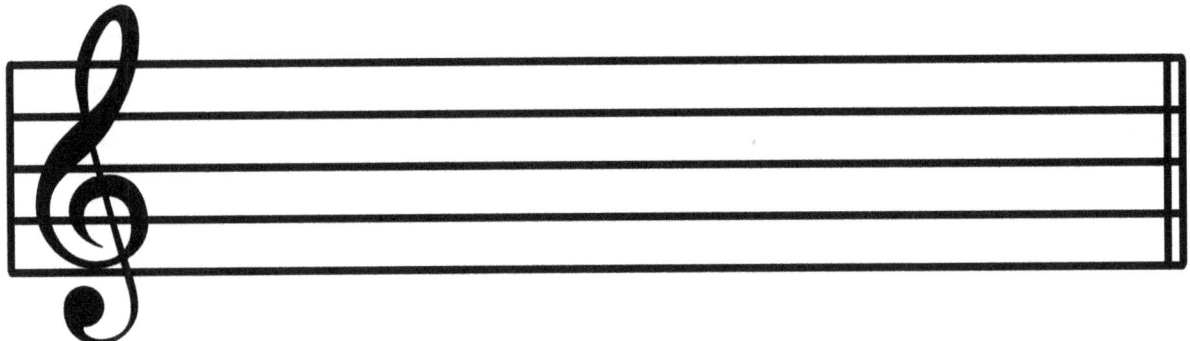

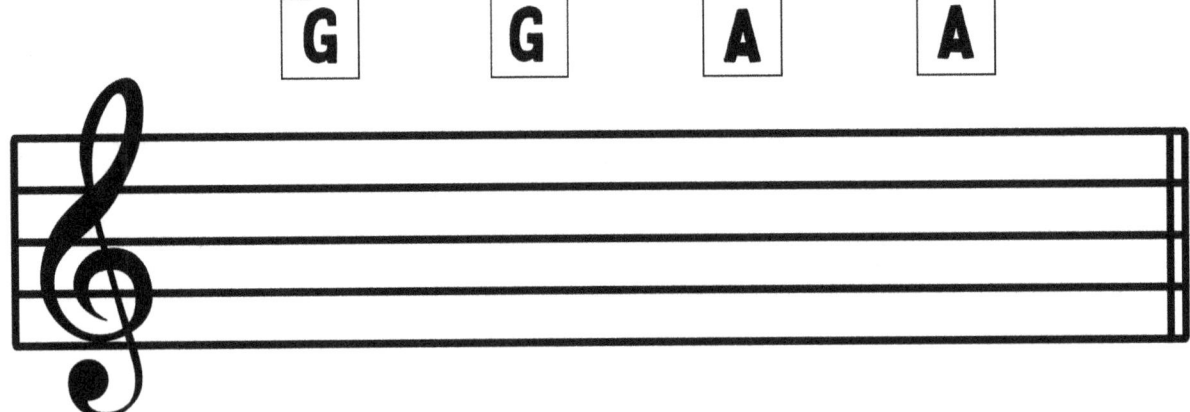

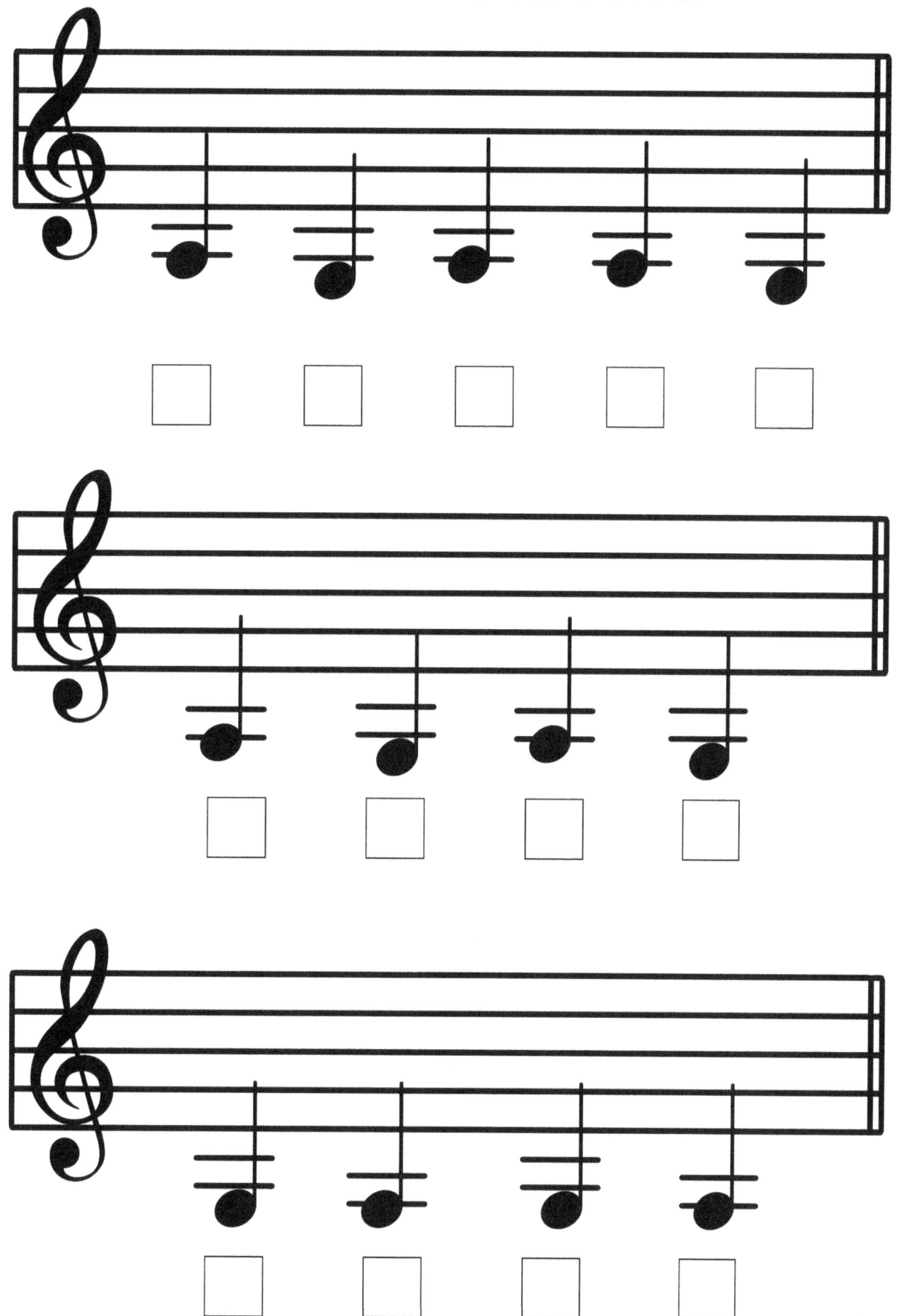

TREBLE G, A & B

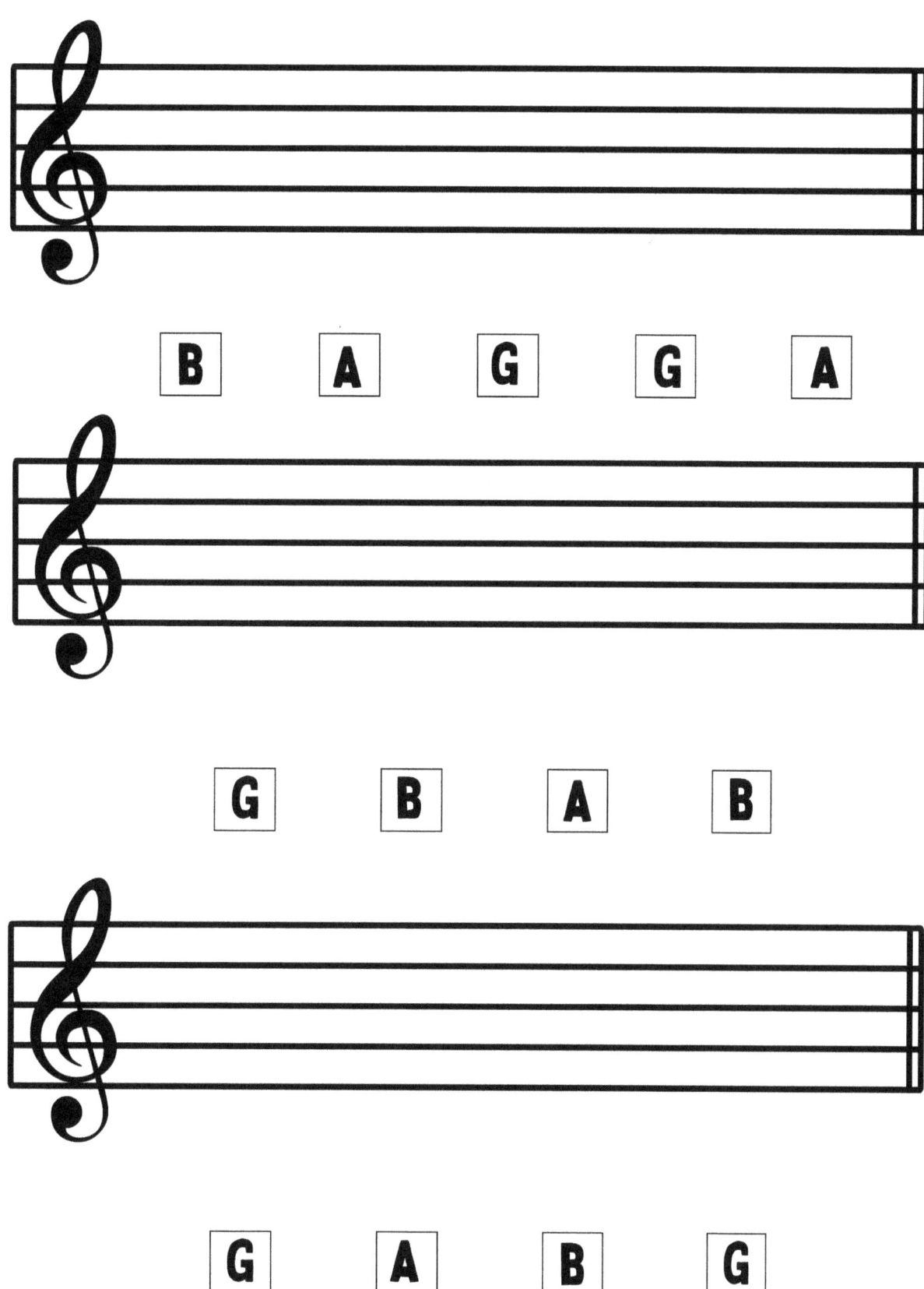

VIOLIN OPEN G, 1, 2 ON G

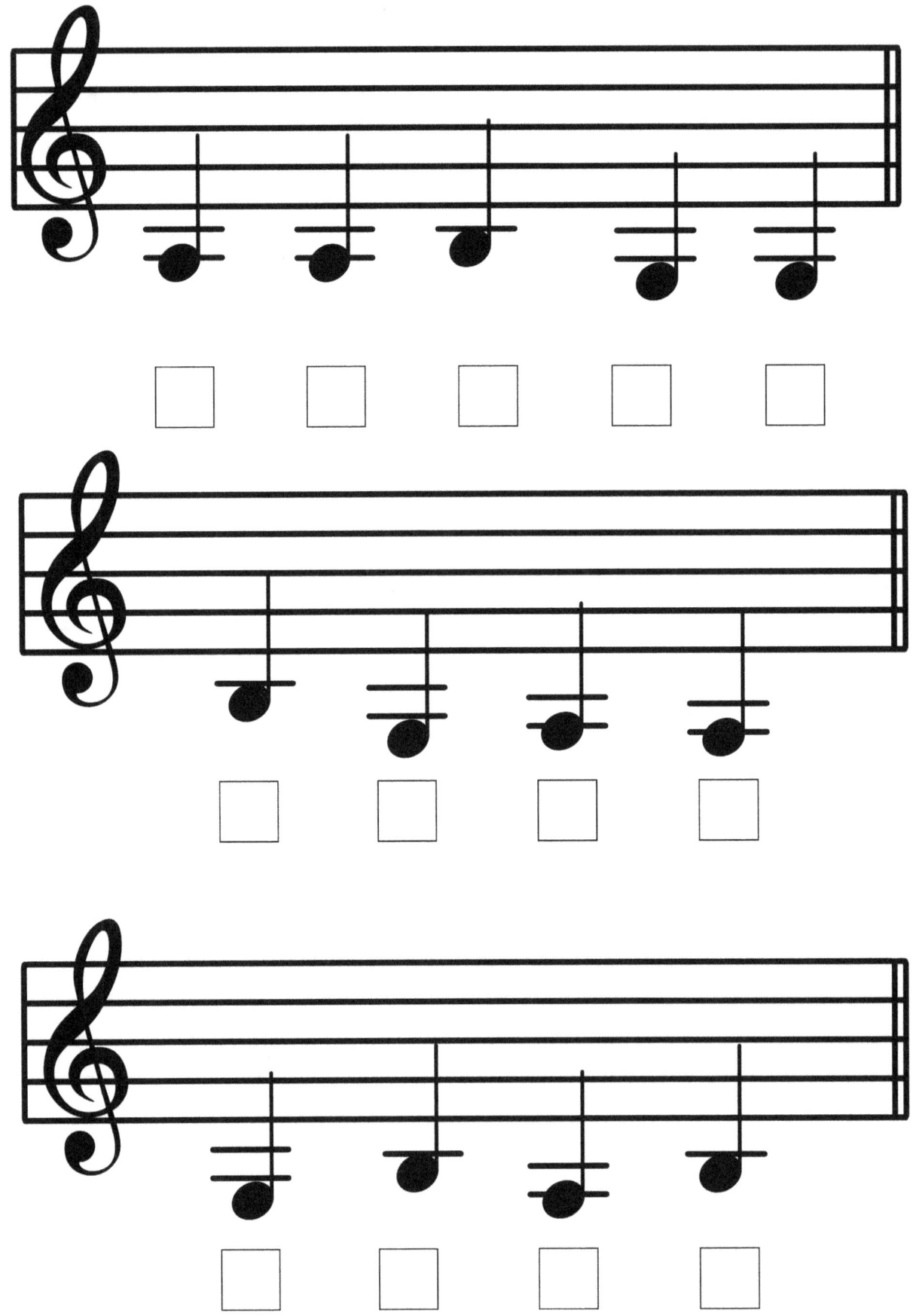

TREBLE G, A, B & C

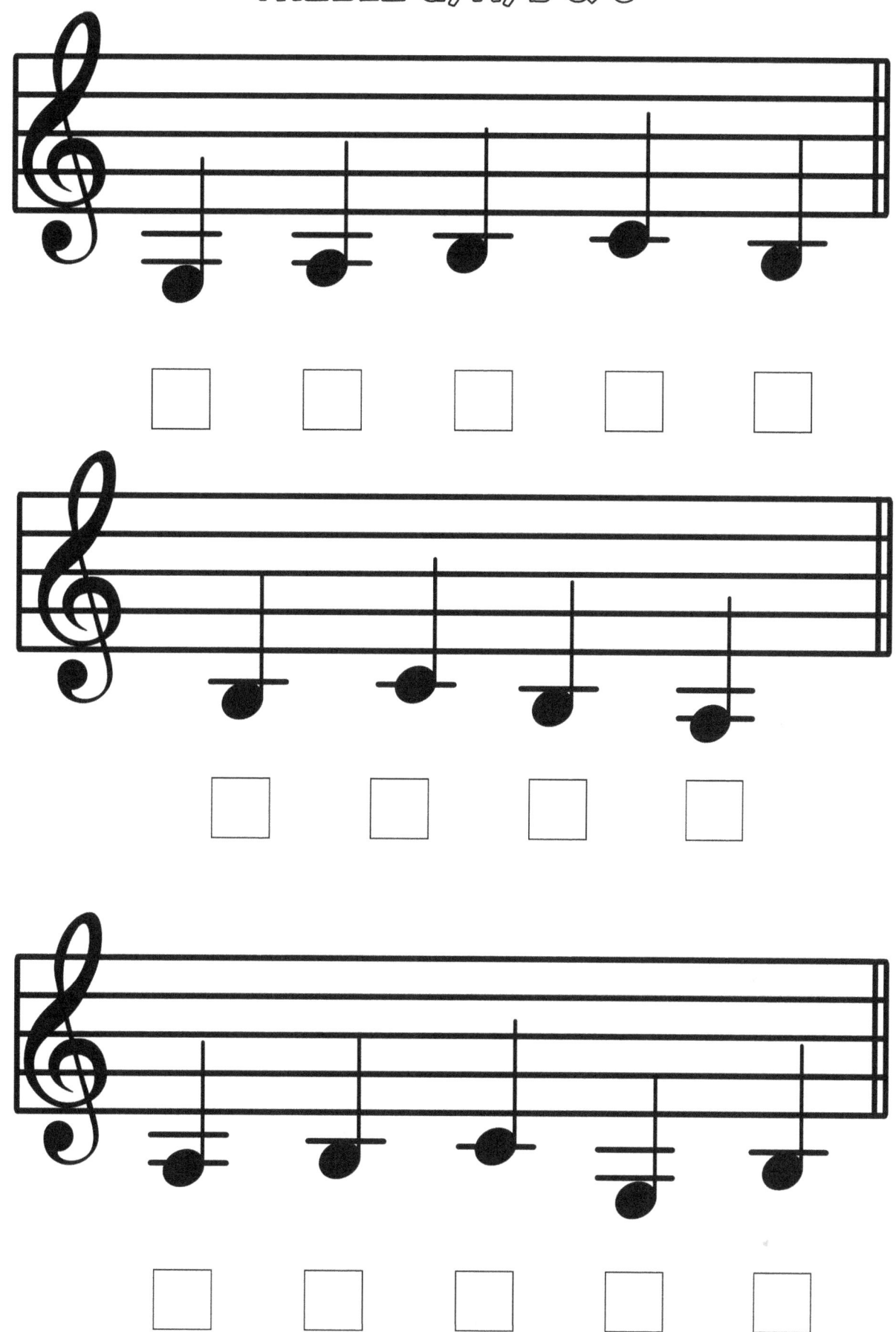

WRITE TREBLE CLEF G, A, B & C

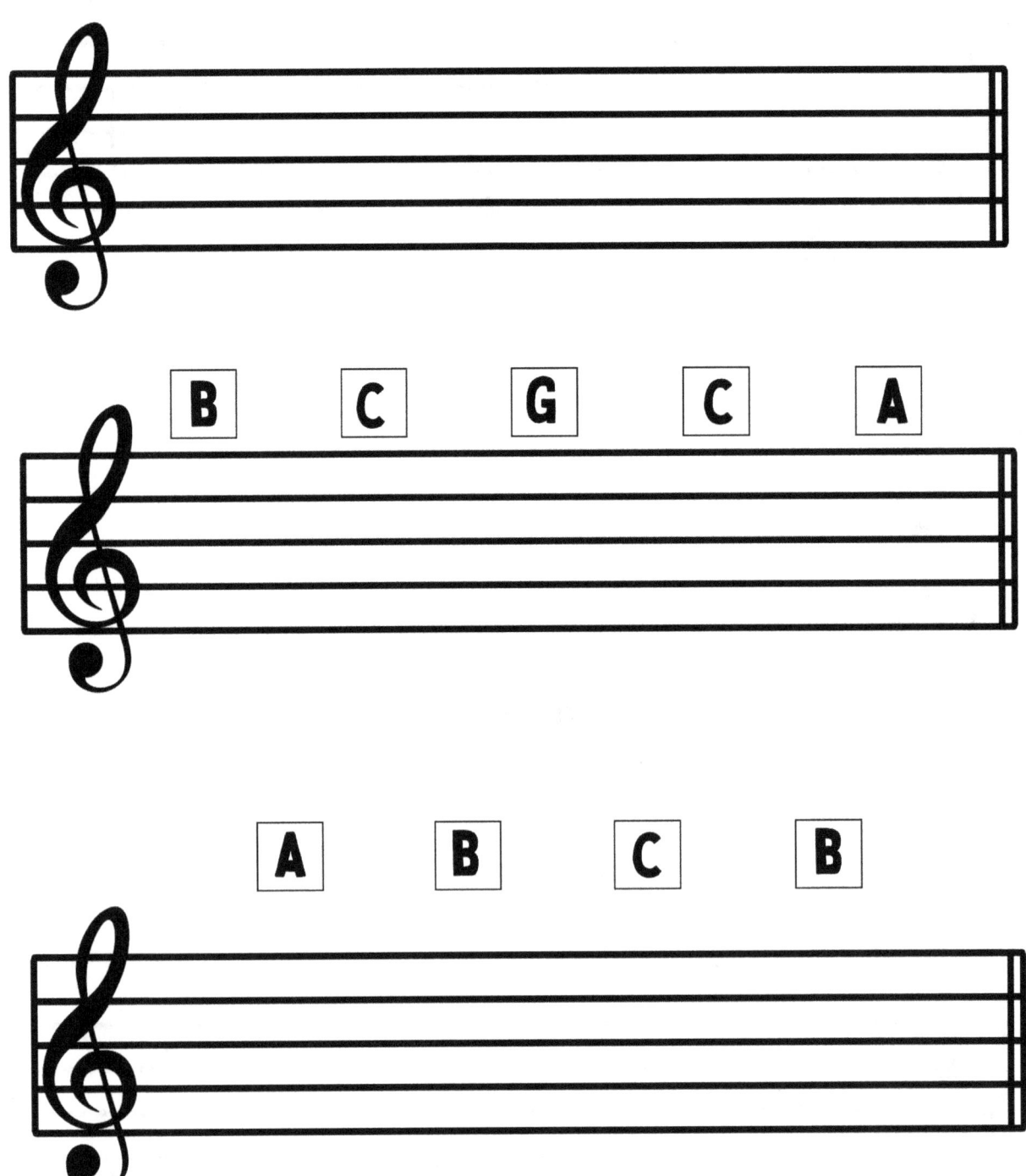

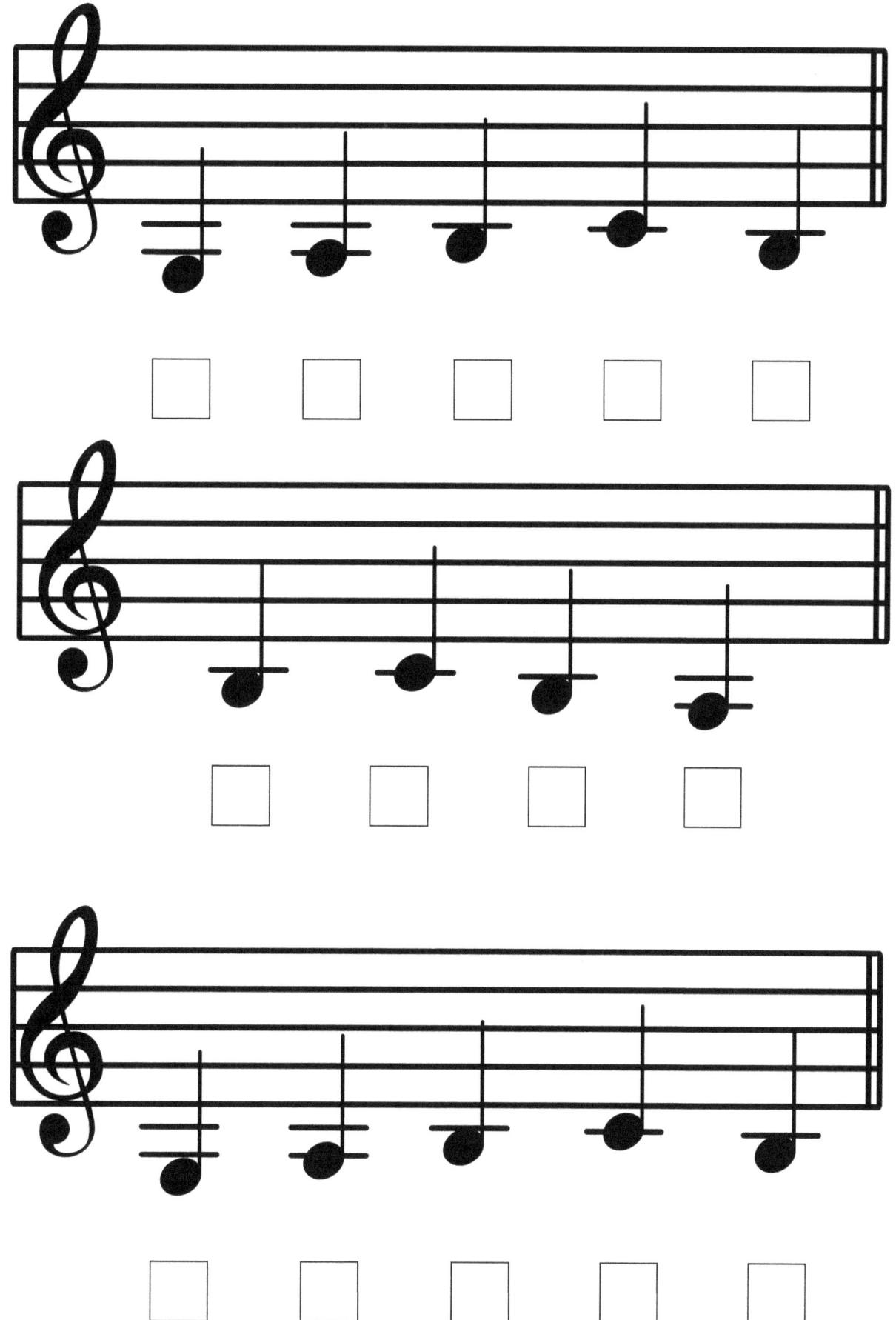

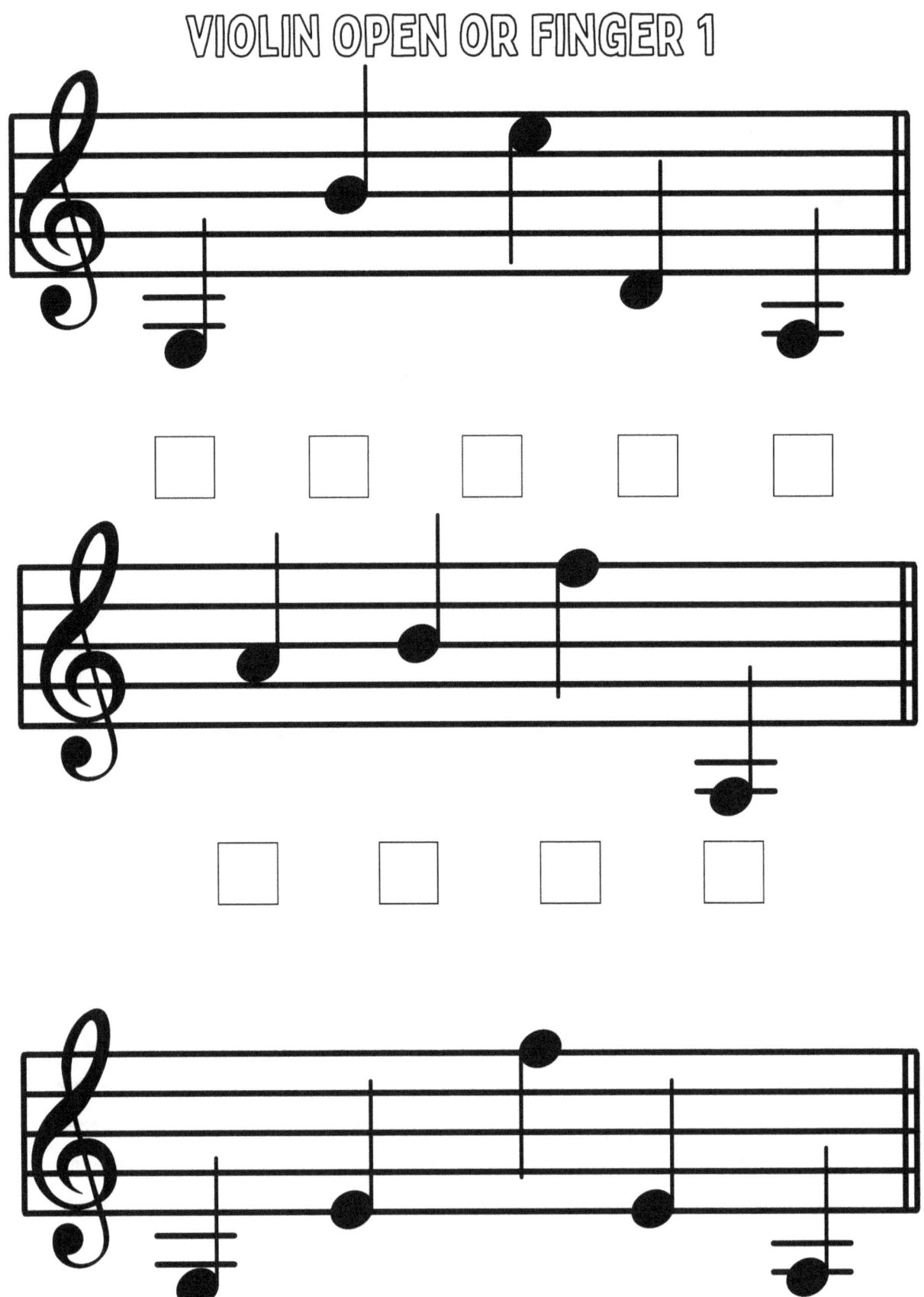

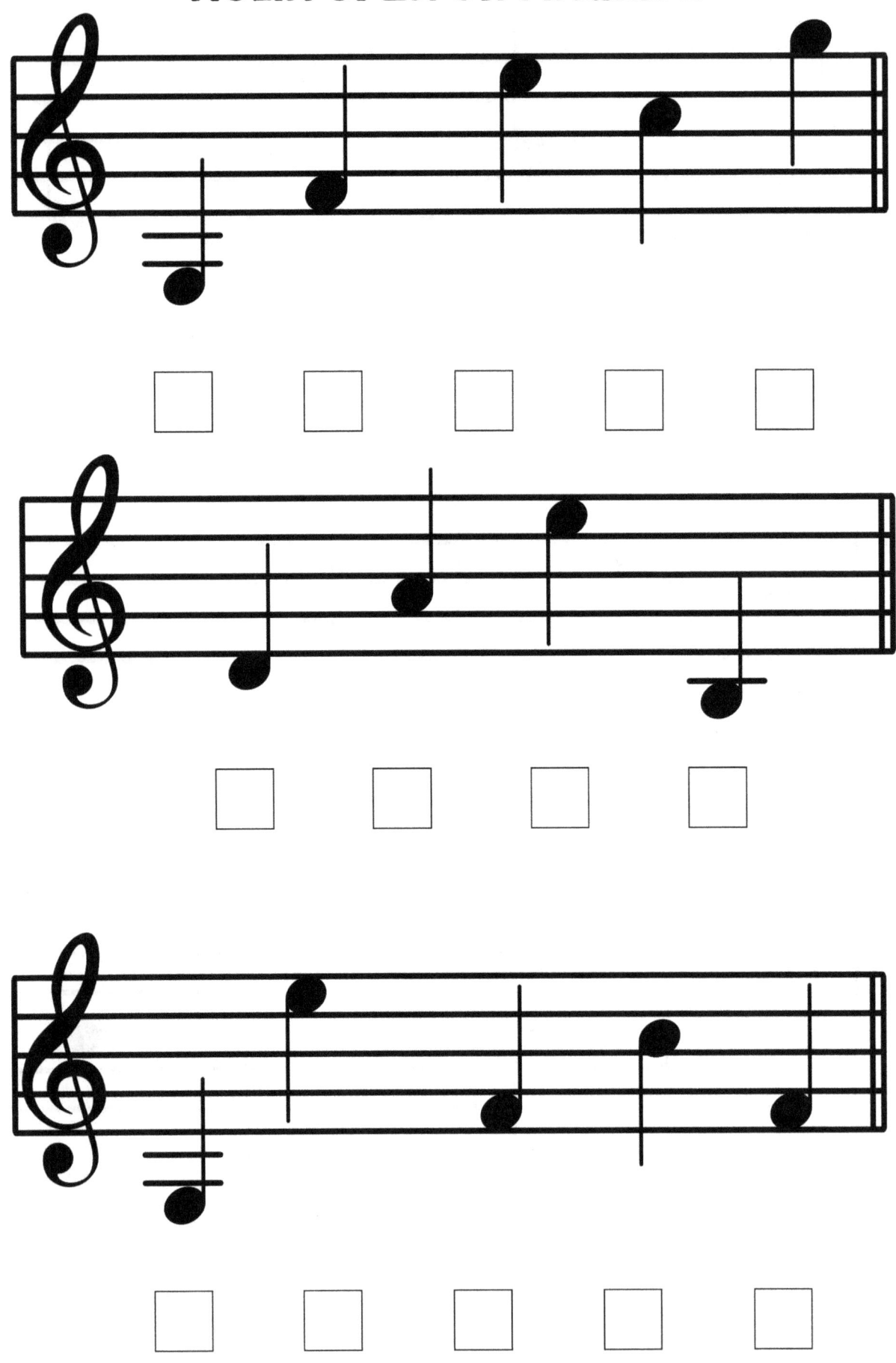

VIOLIN OPEN OR FINGER 2

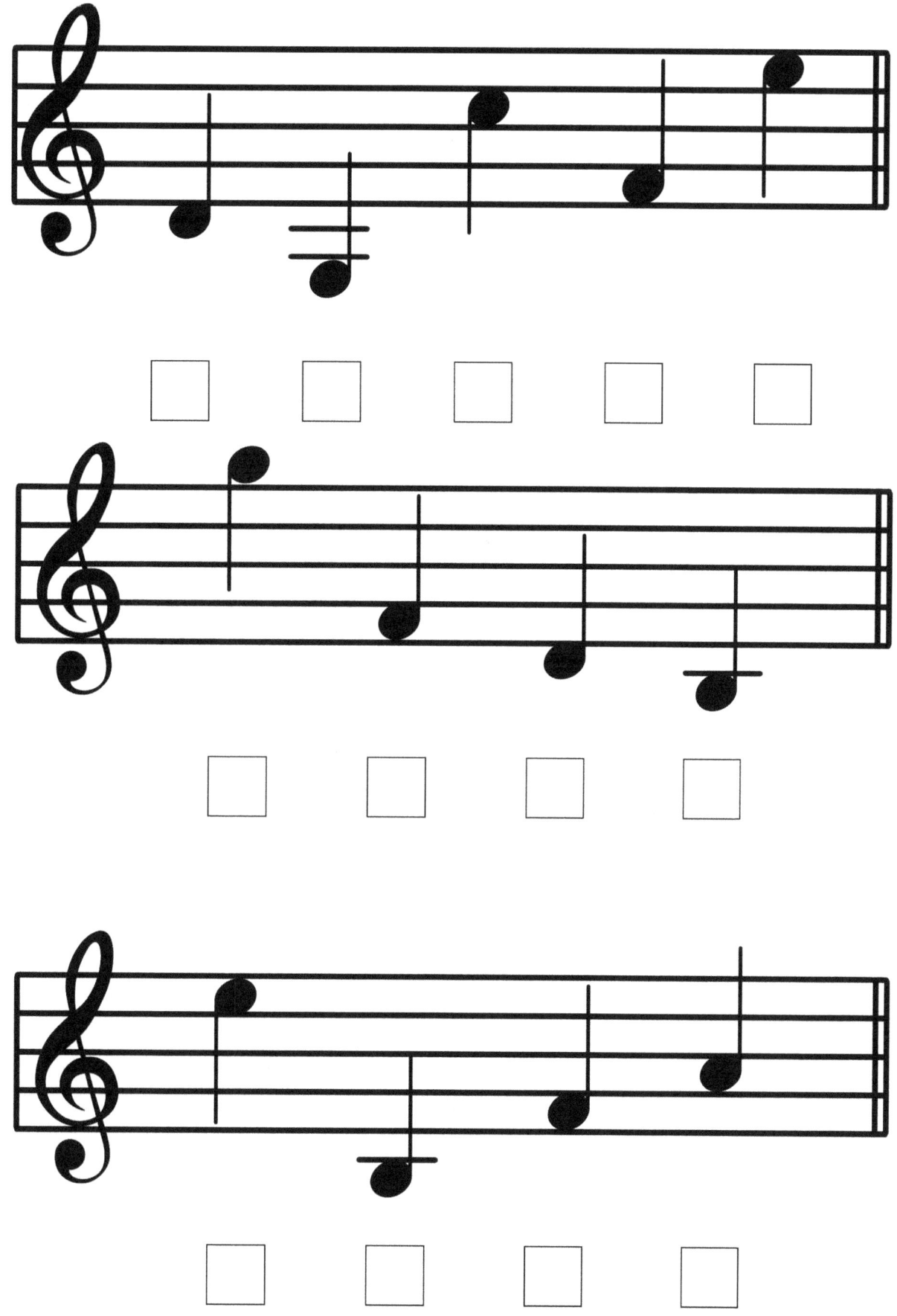

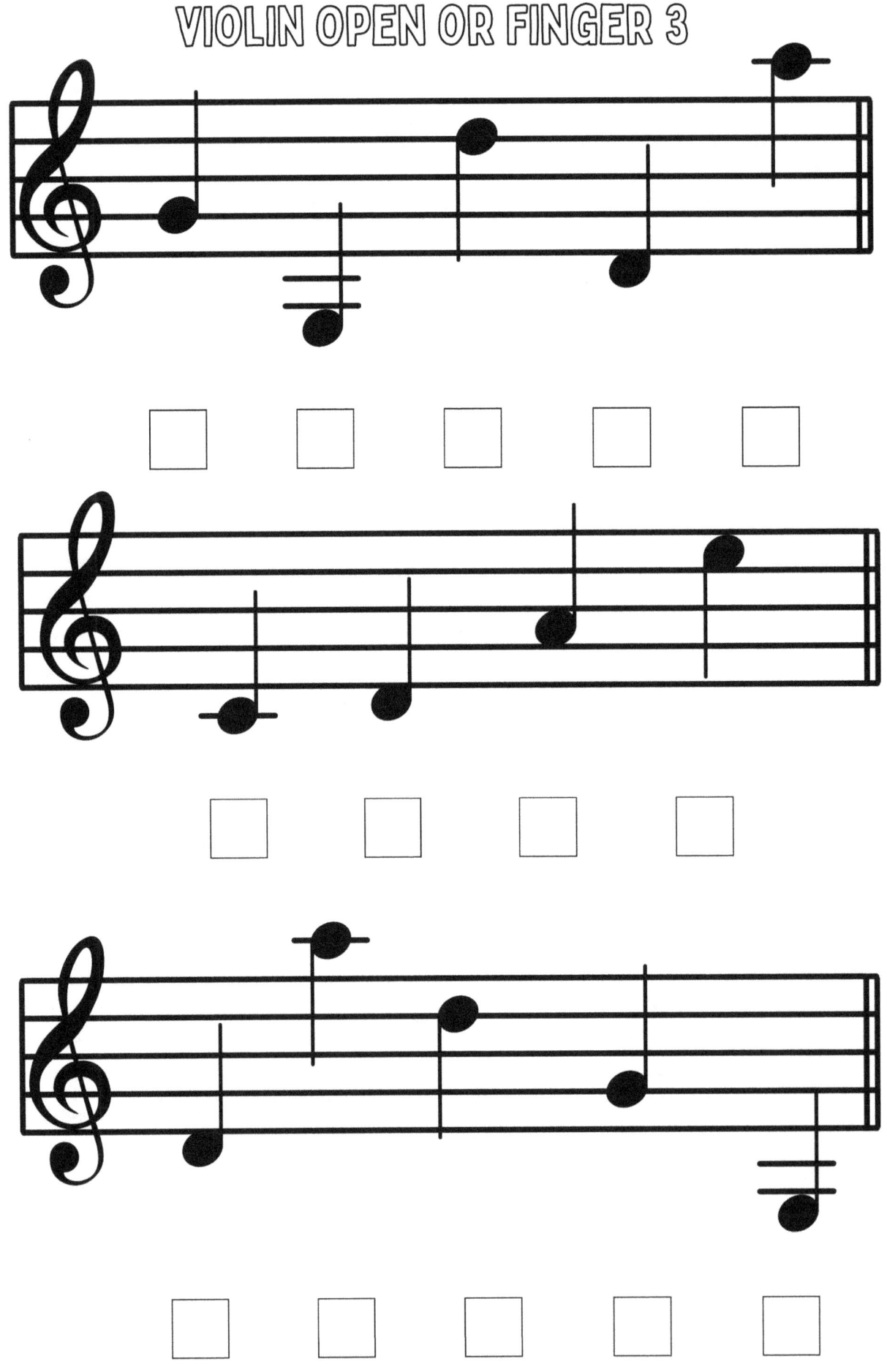

FINGER 1 OR 3

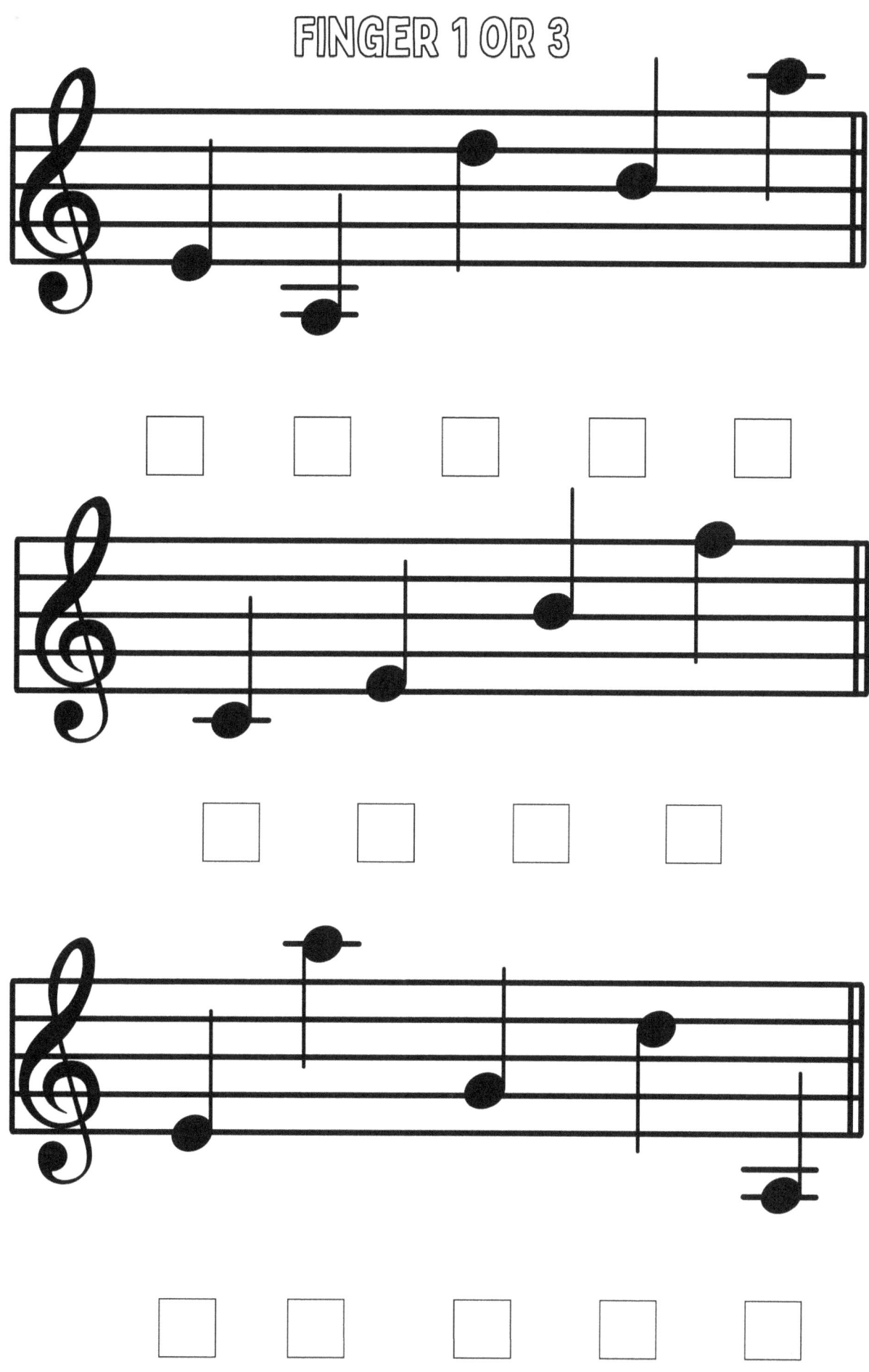

FINGER 2 OR 1

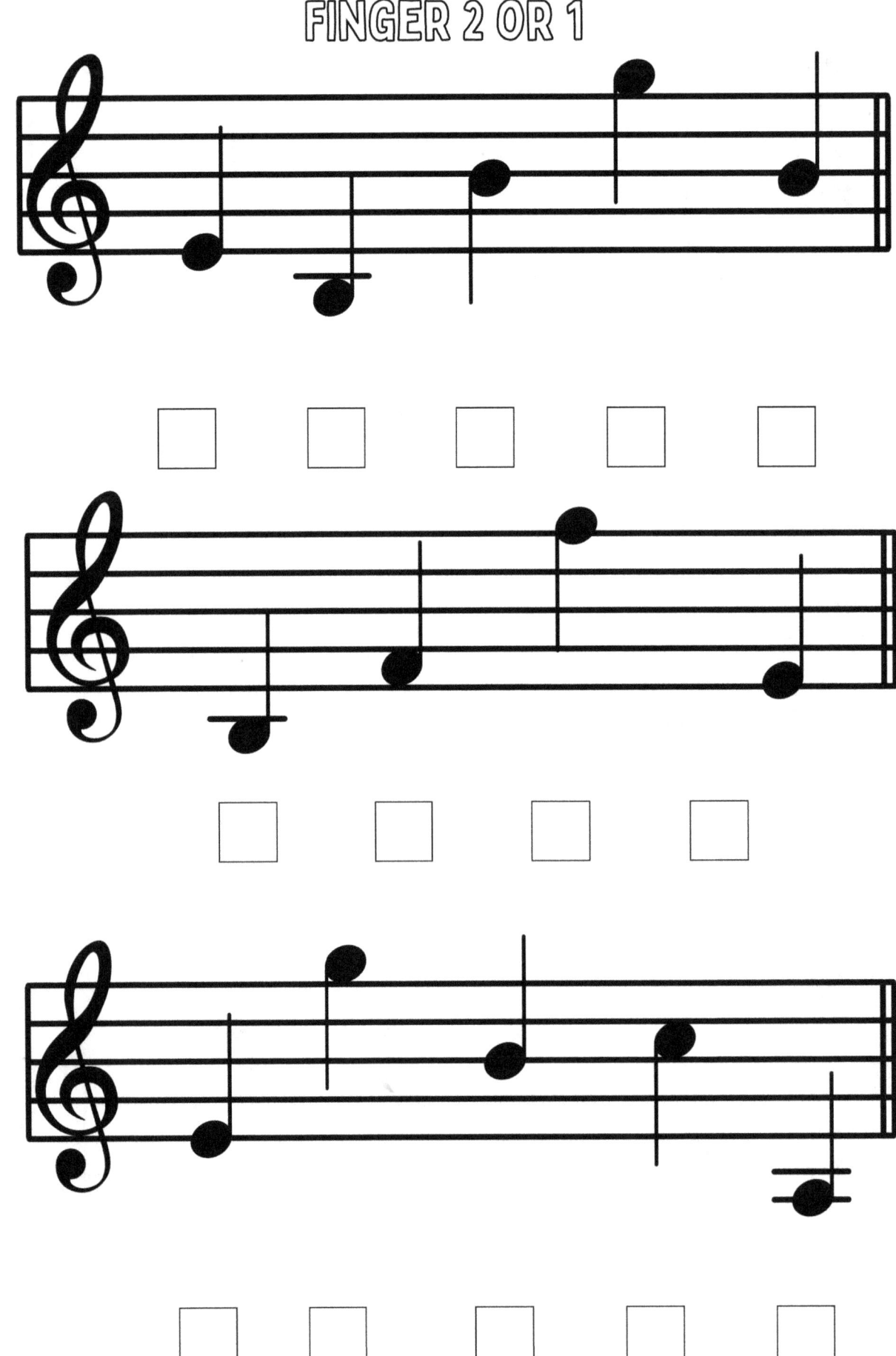

FINGER 2 OR 3

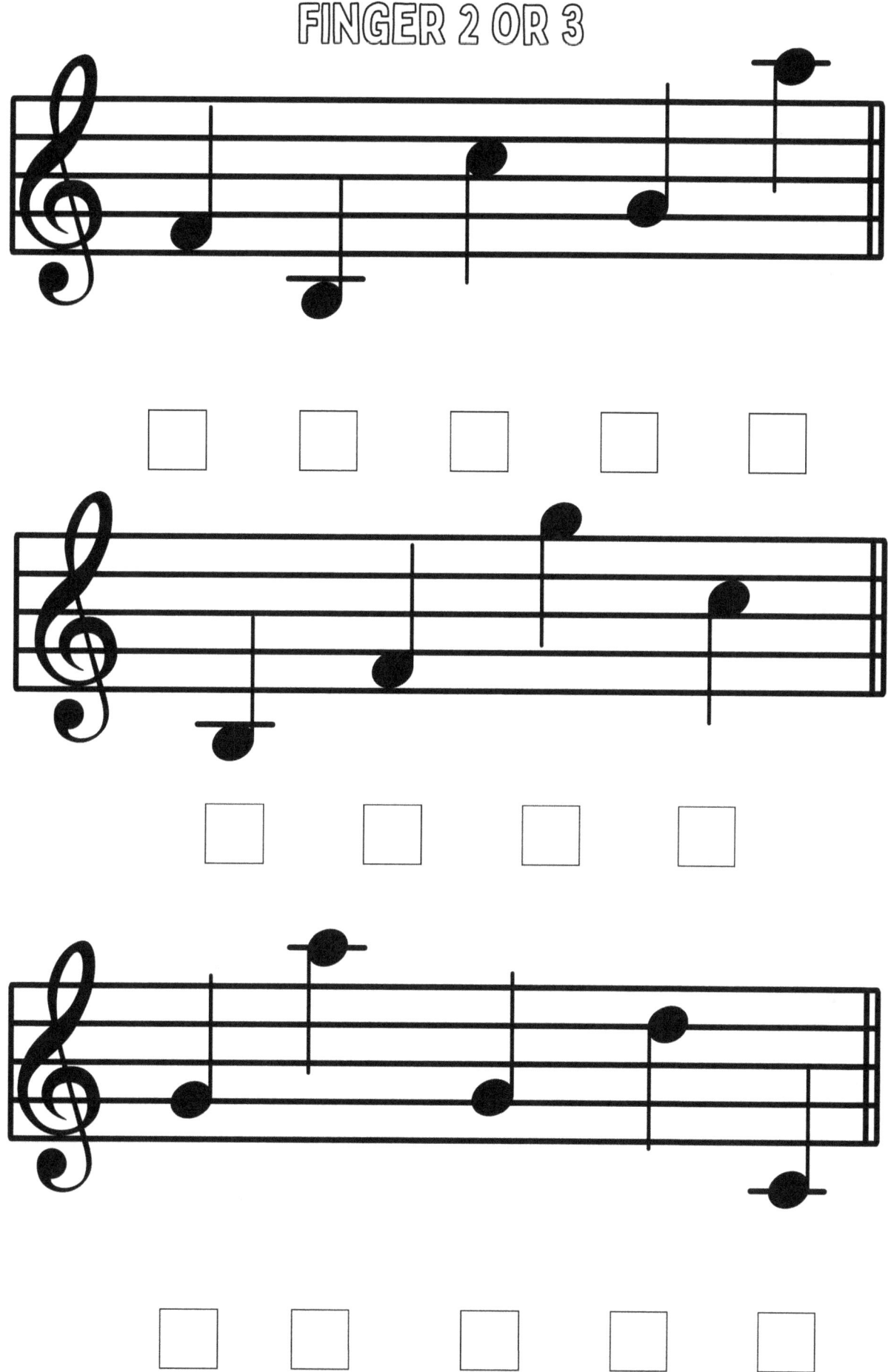

FINGER 1, 2 OR 3

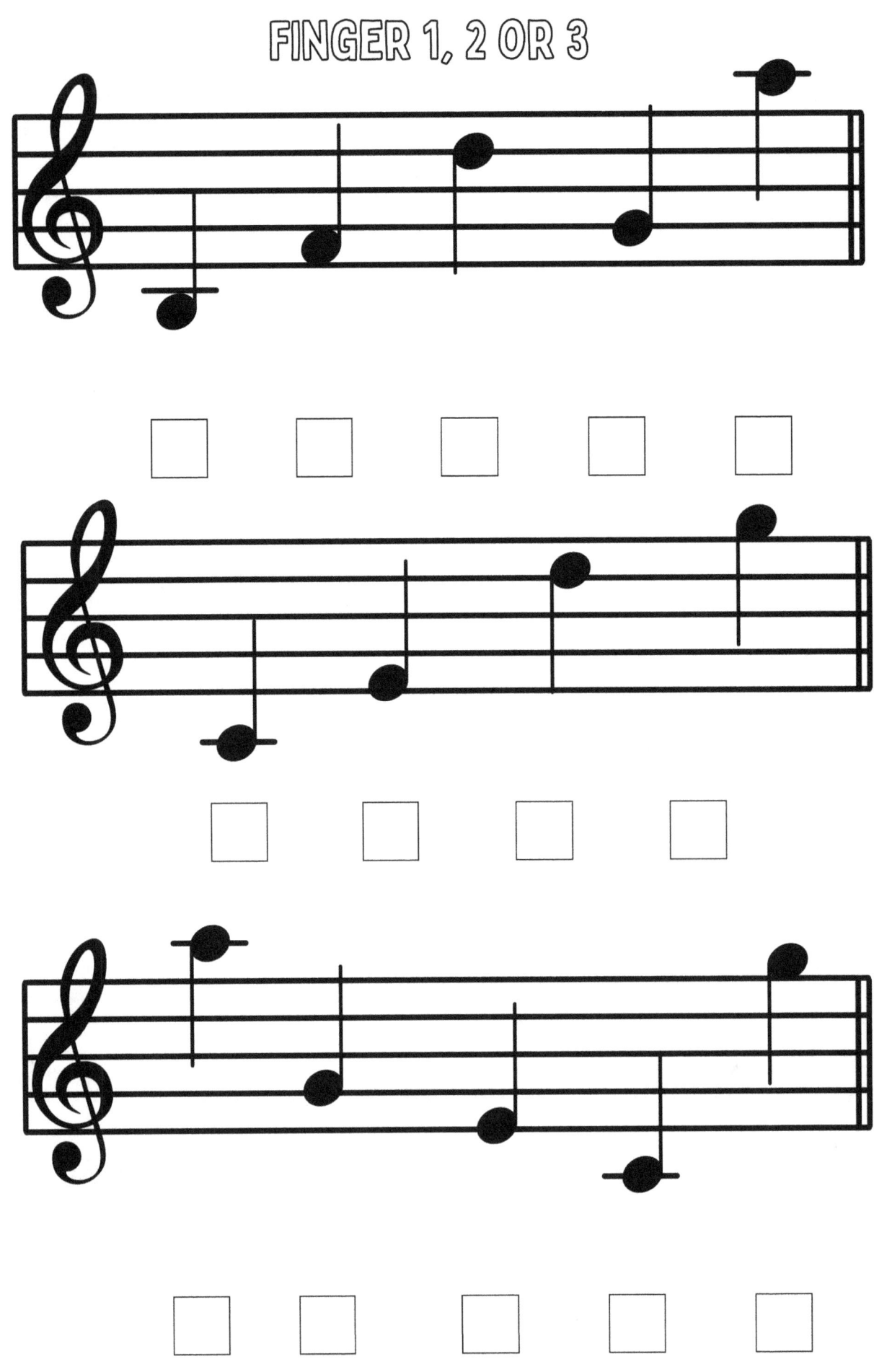

VIOLIN OPEN OR FINGER 3

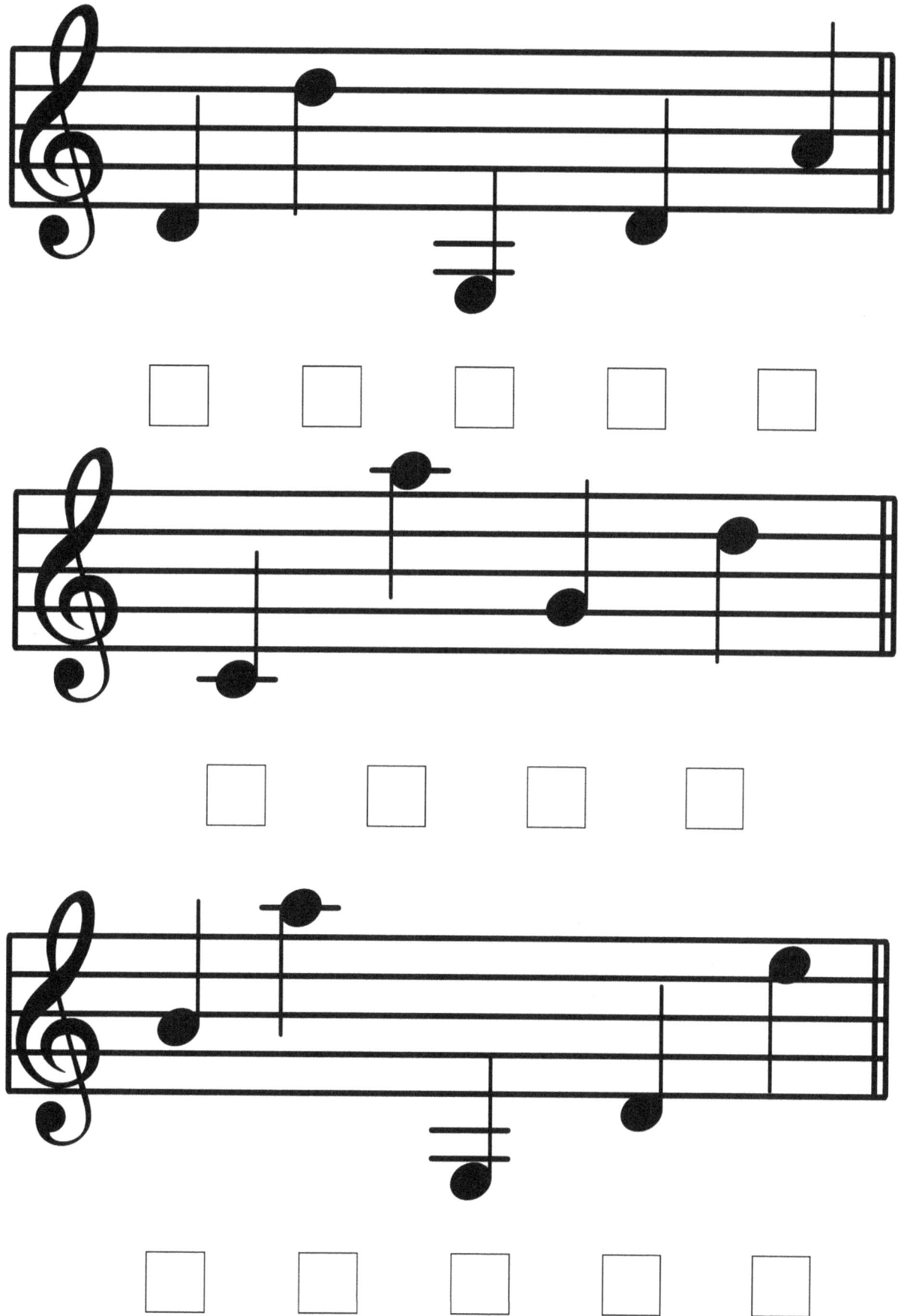

NOTES = WORDS

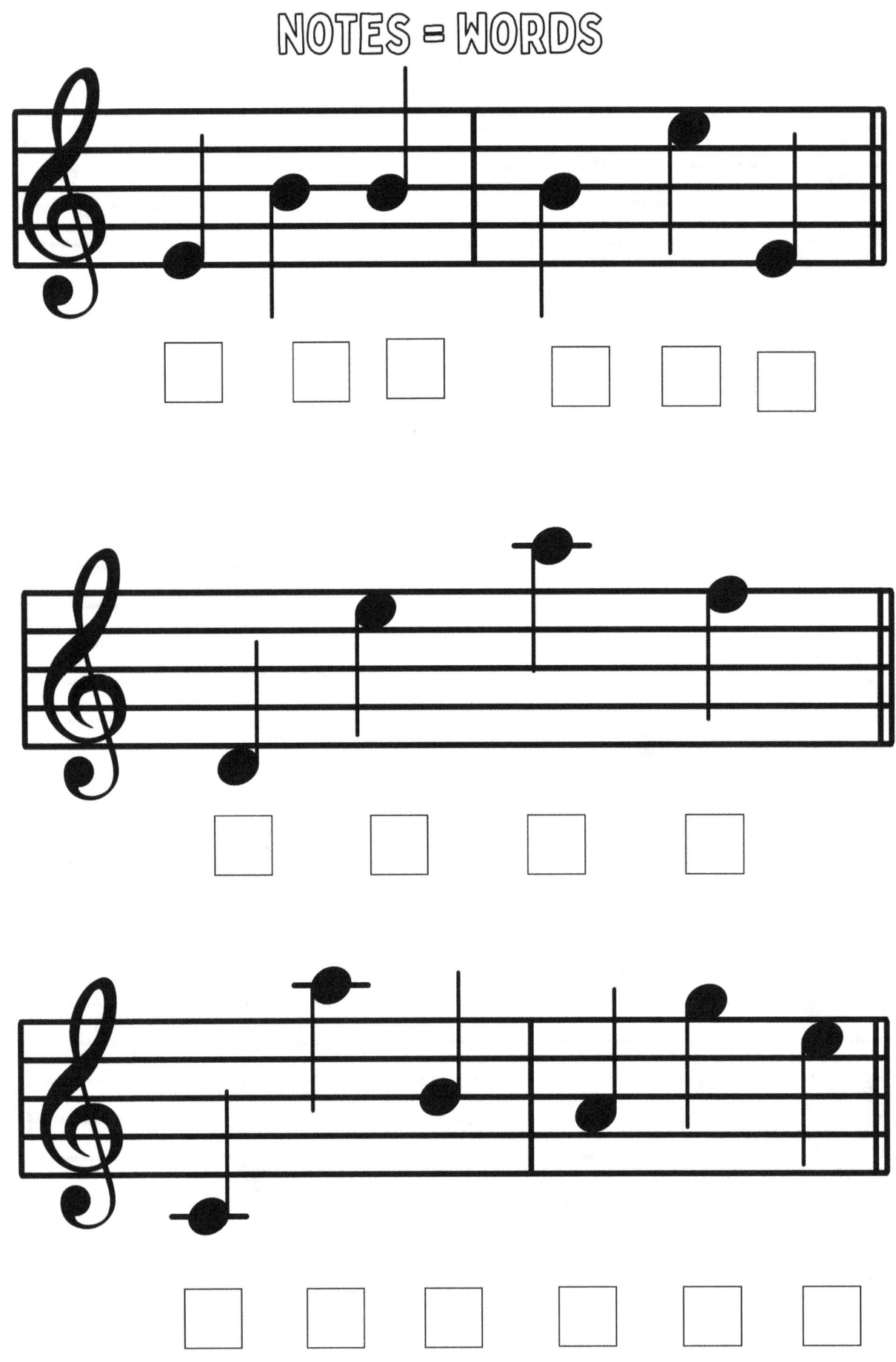

NOTES = WORDS

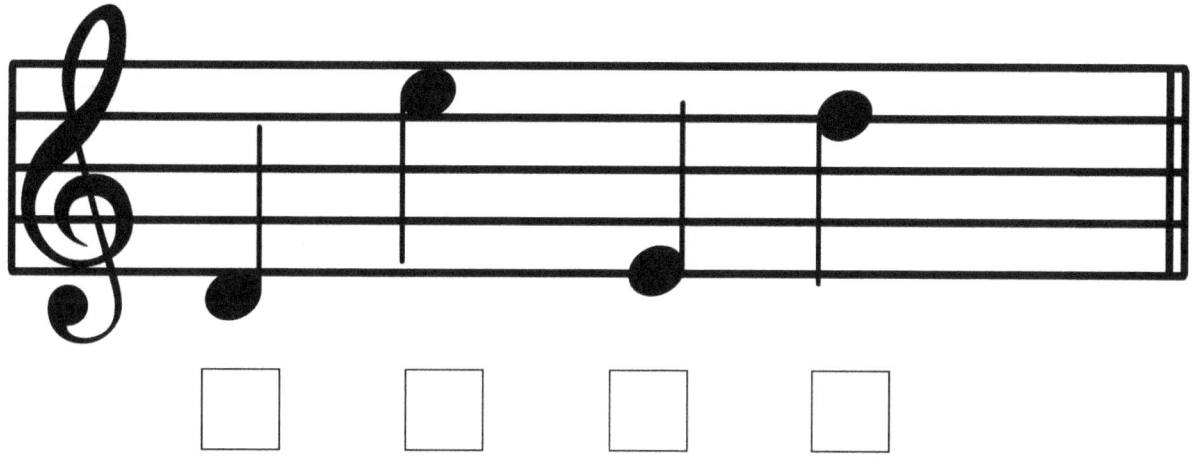

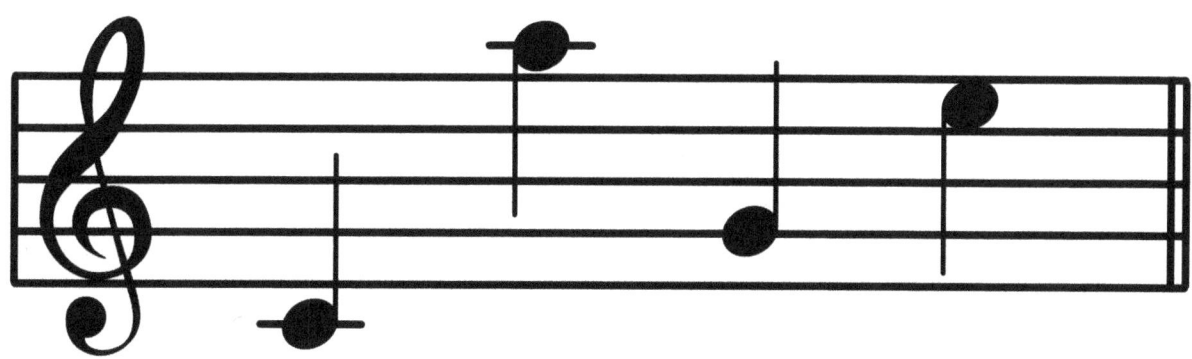

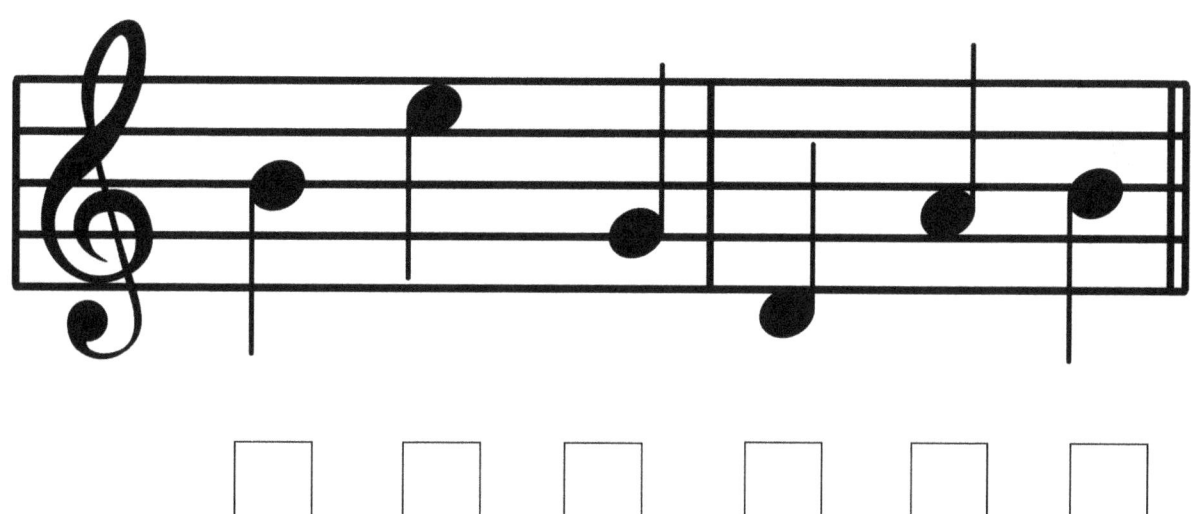

NOTES = WORDS

NOTES = WORDS

NOTES = WORDS

NOTES = WORDS

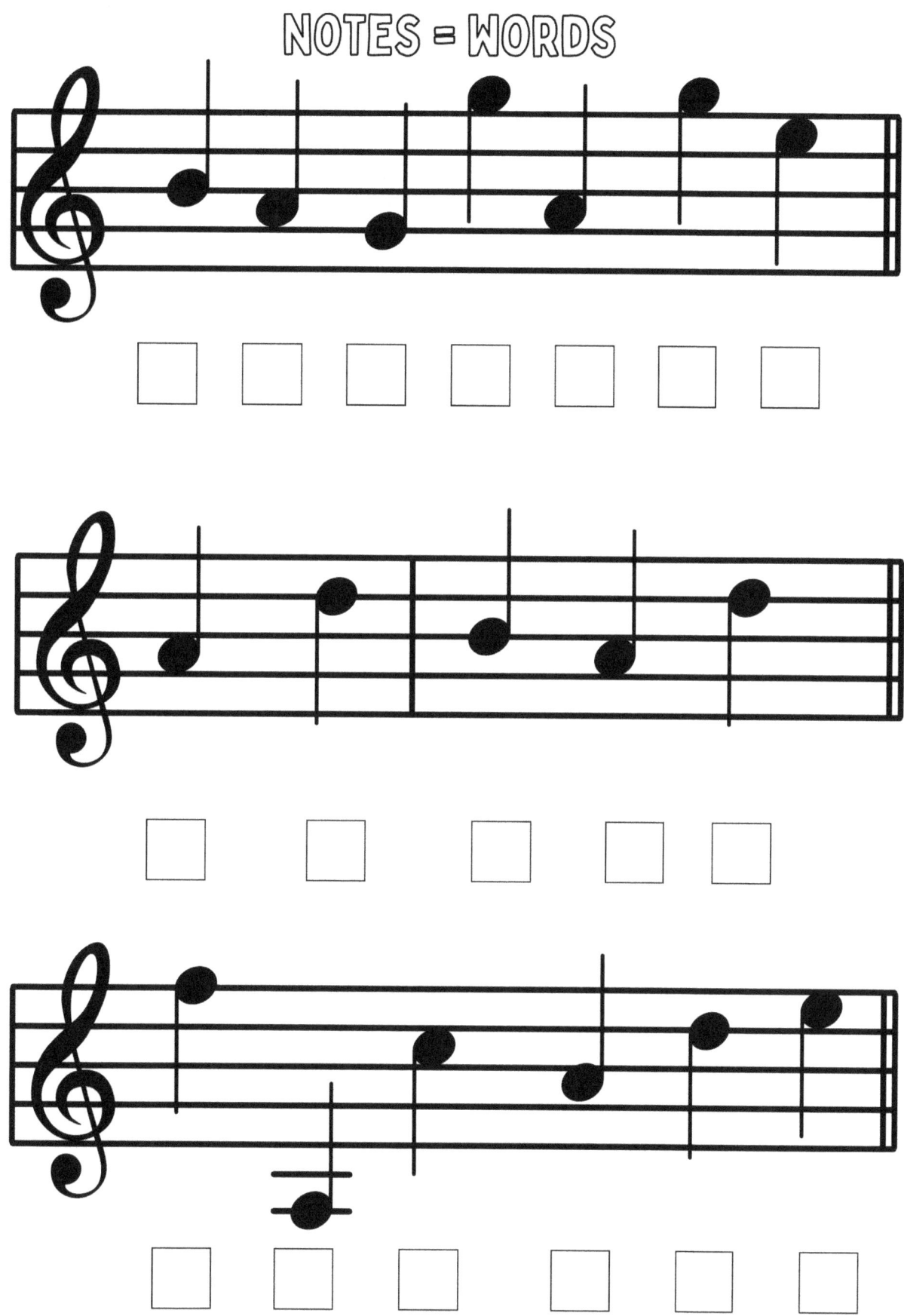

HOW TO BUILD A TREBLE CLEF
FLIP BOOK

1. Ask students to complete the steps to build a treble clef (write and/or draw)

2. When they finish ask them to cut the 5 boxes (pages) of the Flip Book.

3. Tell students to glue or staple the pages together, one onto the other, following the numbers.

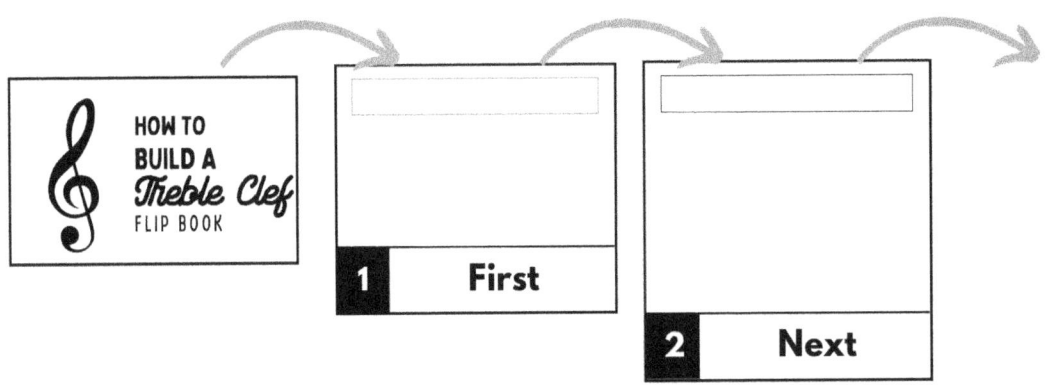

4. The Flip Book will look like this:

5. Finally ask your students to show their books and tell a friend how to build a Treble Clef

HOW TO BUILD A *Treble Clef* FLIP BOOK

GLUE OR STAPLE HERE

1 **FIRST**

GLUE OR STAPLE HERE

2 **Next**

GLUE OR STAPLE HERE

3 **Then**

GLUE OR STAPLE HERE

4 **Last**

1 Complete with the steps to build a treble clef (draw/write).

2 Cut the boxes and glue them in order.

CERTIFICATE
OF ACHIEVEMENT

This awarded to :

----

for the achievement of the completion of:

_____   _____
Teacher   Date

BOOK LEVEL CHART FOR THE **VERY FUN VIOLIN LIBRARY**

VIOLIN GRADE	FUN VIOLIN LEVEL	MAIN CONCEPTS
PRE-TWINKLE	A	RHYTHMS, FINGERS 1,2,3 ON A, FINGER 1 ON E
LEVEL 1A	B	NOTE READING 1,2,3 ON A, OPEN D & 1 ON E
LEVEL 1B	C	NOTE READING ON D, A & E STRINGS, FINGER 4
LEVEL 2A	D	NOTE READING ON ALL STRINGS
LEVEL 2B	E	INTRO TO 3RD POSITION & VIBRATO

C. JUDY NAILLON 2020 WWW.VIOLINJUDY.COM

Mrs. Judy Naillon, or "ViolinJudy" is a dedicated and enthusiastic independent piano and violin teacher, composer, and professional violinist. Her work consists of her large private music studio, as well as playing with her string quartet and Wichita Symphony Orchestra. She served as a church musician for over 20 years and is active in leadership in the musicians' union. She loves coming up with creative ideas to help both students and teachers be successful and blogs about it all at www.ViolinJudy.com and for Alfred's Music Publishers. When she is not writing new Violin books she loves spending time with her family and little dog Pom.

www.ingramcontent.com/pod-product-compliance
Lightning Source LLC
Chambersburg PA
CBHW081019040426
42444CB00014B/3276